Southern Arizona's Most Haunted

Renée Gardner

*Happy Hauntings
Renee*

4880 Lower Valley Road, Atglen, Pennsylvania 19310

Ouija is a registered trademark of Parker Brothers Games
text by Renee Gardner
photos by Renee Gardner unless noted otherwise in the text

Copyright © 2010 by Renée Gardner
Library of Congress Control Number: 2009939989
    All rights reserved. No part of this work may be reproduced or used in any form or by any means—graphic, electronic, or mechanical, including photocopying or information storage and retrieval systems—without written permission from the publisher.
    The scanning, uploading and distribution of this book or any part thereof via the Internet or via any other means without the permission of the publisher is illegal and punishable by law. Please purchase only authorized editions and do not participate in or encourage the electronic piracy of copyrighted materials.
    "Schiffer," "Schiffer Publishing Ltd. & Design," and the "Design of pen and ink well" are registered trademarks of Schiffer Publishing Ltd.
Designed by "Sue"
Type set in IceAge/New Baskerville BT
ISBN: 978-0-7643-3416-0
Printed in The United States of America

Schiffer Books are available at special discounts for bulk purchases for sales promotions or premiums. Special editions, including personalized covers, corporate imprints, and excerpts can be created in large quantities for special needs. For more information contact the publisher:

Published by Schiffer Publishing Ltd.
4880 Lower Valley Road, Atglen, PA 19310
Phone: (610) 593-1777; Fax: (610) 593-2002
E-mail: Info@schifferbooks.com

For the largest selection of fine reference books on this and related subjects, please visit our web site at **www.schifferbooks.com**
We are always looking for people to write books on new and related subjects.
If you have an idea for a book please contact us at the above address.

This book may be purchased from the publisher.
Include $5.00 for shipping.
Please try your bookstore first.
You may write for a free catalog.

In Europe, Schiffer books are distributed by
Bushwood Books
6 Marksbury Ave.
Kew Gardens
Surrey TW9 4JF England
Phone: 44 (0) 20 8392-8585; Fax: 44 (0) 20 8392-9876
E-mail: info@bushwoodbooks.co.uk
Website: www.bushwoodbooks.co.uk

Dedication

This book is dedicated to everyone who has helped me gather stories, information, and experiences about the paranormal. I would also like to dedicate this book to my parents who never said there were no such things as ghosts, and to my sister who brought our ghost home from school. To Peter, my husband, who is the biggest skeptic, but my biggest supporter. I would especially like to thank Gizmo, my biggest fan!

Acknowledgments

I would like to thank the following people for sharing their stories with us for the book and our tours: Denyse Leventman, Jeff DiGregorio and Chuck Bressi, Carlos, LeRoy, Nova, Linda and Lacey, Brenna and Moses Mercer, Phil, Audrey Campbell, Kevin, Connie, Dan, Kathy, Adam, Rita, Leigha, Sean, Steven and Stephen and everyone else at the Copper Queen Hotel for letting me invade your establishment every Thursday night to search for the spirits that haunt it, David Smith, Ilona, Nancy Jacobson, Donna and David at the Source Within, Christy from ICPIR and her entire team, the City of Bisbee, the City of Tombstone, the City of Tucson, and everyone who does not throw rocks at us.

I'd also like to thank Vince, LeeAnn, Marge and Stephen Elliot, Barbara, Jenn, Ed, Jen and Justin at the Shady Dell, Fiona, Mitch, Suzanne, and their daughters, and Ted for their stories.

Contents

Introduction 7
   Who am I? 7
   What are Ghosts? 11

Tucson 13
   A Brief History of Tucson 14
   St. Augustine's Cathedral 15
   Scottish Rite Building 17
   Santa Rita Hotel 19
   Tucson Railroad Depot and Transportation
      Museum 21
   Pioneer International Hotel 23
   Fox Theater 26
   Hotel Congress 28
   Royal Elizabeth Bed and Breakfast 32
   The Manning House 34

Tombstone 36
   A Brief History of Tombstone 37
   OK Corral 38
   Historic Tombstone Courthouse 40
   Schieffelin Hall 42
   Bella Union Building 45
   Corner of 1st and Toughnut 48
   Big Nose Kate's 51
   Corner of 5th and Allen 54
   Charleston Rd 56
   Aztec House 58
   Buford House 60

Western Heritage Museum 62
Milton House 66
Brunckow's Cabin 68
Red Buffalo Trading Company 69
Crystal Palace 70
Bird Cage Theatre 72

Bisbee 84

A Brief History of Bisbee 85
Bisbee Grand Hotel 86
Inn at Castle Rock 92
Oliver House 94
Bisbee Inn/Hotel LaMore 98
City Park 105
St Elmo Bar 108
OK Street Boarding House 110
Bisbee Courthouse 112
Brewery Gulch Brothel 114
Audrey's Inn 115
Bisbee Repertory Theater 117
Bisbee Convention Center 118
Mitchel Family Mortuary 119
Silver King Hotel 122
Opera Drive Brothel 123
Hotel San Ramon 124
Shady Dell 127
Eldorado Suites 130
Copper Queen Hotel 132

So You Want To Be a Ghost Hunter 143

Bibliography 157

Introduction

Who Am I?

On my ghost tours I am asked almost every night how I got into studying the paranormal and collecting ghost stories. The answer is not a quick or easy one and goes all the way back to my childhood.

I grew up in a haunted house in the suburbs of Philadelphia. Through my bedroom was access to the attic. At night I could tell something was there, watching me. I would hide under the covers until I scared myself to sleep, too afraid to poke my head out in case something really had manifested itself there for my eyes to witness.

My mother experienced most of the paranormal activity. Pots and pans would come out of the kitchen cupboards and with thunderous noise end up in the middle of the kitchen floor, toilets would flush by themselves, the front doorbell would ring and thirty seconds later the back doorbell would ring—of course no one was at either door. Important items would be placed somewhere specific, disappear, and then reappear in a different location.

A Resident Haunt

We knew we had a resident ghost that decided to take our home as his or her own. At the time the haunting began, my sister was in the fourth grade at Penn Wynne Elementary School, and her classroom had a pet ghost named George Hossenfefer. We believed that the playful spirit came home with my sister one day and took up residence in our house—or at least this was the story our parents told my sister and me to keep us from being too scared. From then on we referred to the spirit as George Hossenfefer.

When I was a teenager, my parents added an addition onto the house, and in doing so, took off the attic to add another floor. Usually construction on a haunted building stirs up paranormal activity, but our case was rare in that it caused George Hossenfefer to calm down or, as some family members believe, to move on to another dwelling.

He remained quiet through my high school years and up until after I had long moved out and graduated college. My sister had moved out of the house as well by that time.

The activity started up again nineteen years after it began. On one occasion, my mother swept and mopped the floors in the kitchen late at night. The next morning when she came down to make breakfast, it appeared that someone had already been there and helped themselves to food, leaving the evidence in crumbs all over the kitchen floor. On another night, she swept the kitchen floor before going to bed. The next morning, she woke up and went down to the kitchen only to find that during the night some unseen visitor had tracked dirt from her garden throughout the room. Other occurrences included TV channels changing by themselves and lights turning themselves off.

When I was in the eighth grade, my friend, Jamie, and I decided to play with the Ouija board. She felt that her grandmother was haunting her house. Her grandmother used to live with her and her family and died in one of the rooms in the home. We went into the room, set up the Ouija board and candles on a little table and tried to make contact. This was a very stupid thing to try to do. We were young, ignorant, and did not understand the powers that could come through the use of the Ouija board. We "played" with the board for a few hours, and after getting bored we blew out all the candles, left the board out and went downstairs to watch TV.

A couple of minutes later the smoke detectors upstairs were going off. We ran upstairs with Jamie's mother leading us as fast as she could. The table that we used to play with the Ouija board was now on fire. Engulfed with flames, Jamie's mother picked it up and dumped it in the bathtub; she turned the shower on to extinguish the flames. Needless to say, this was the last time I have ever used the Ouija board, and would highly discourage anyone from using one!

For Rent: Haunted Apartment

I went to college at OTIS College of Art and Design in Los Angeles California. The entire campus moved from the MacArthur Park area of Los Angeles (which I might add is much scarier than any ghost I have ever encountered!) to Westchester where LAX is located. I spent half my time at the Westchester campus and half my time in the Downtown's Fashion Campus. I decided to get an apartment in Sherman Oaks, which was affordable and a forty-five-minute commute to either of the campuses. The apartment building was a new three-story-high square-shaped building with a little courtyard in the middle. The courtyard had a pool, hot tub, and BBQs for its residents' delight.

Little did I know that the apartment building I had moved into had been built on the same location as a building that suffered great damage during the Northridge Earthquake in 1994. Due to the earthquake, one of the building's walls completely fell to the ground and the entire apartment building had to be evacuated and then demolished. The manager of the new building was never comfortable talking about the quake, and therefore, I never found out if anyone had perished as a result of the building's wall collapsing. What I *did* know was that my apartment was haunted. Maybe it was the spirit of someone who lived in the building before, or maybe it was the spirit of someone who perished in the quake. Either way, there were so many unexplained phenomena, it couldn't go unnoticed.

The most memorable incidents were during the hot summer months in the San Fernando Valley. To save money, I had put a fan by my open window and turned off the air conditioning. I would do this overnight as I slept to allow some of the cool night air to enter my apartment. On numerous occasions, when I woke up in the morning, the fan would be in a different location then where I left it the night before.

Another memorable experience from that apartment building on Sepulveda Boulevard was the night I witnessed what some call a Shadow Person. I was having a bad dream and awoke to what appeared to be a dark mass holding my arms down by the side of my head. I couldn't move, couldn't scream, couldn't breath. It got up off of me, walked to my bedroom door and vanished into the hallway. Most people would say that what happened to me was sleep paralysis, which is commonly known as Old Hag Syndrome. It used to be believed that an evil old hag was the cause for people to wake up without being able to move or scream for help. My case was a little different because I saw the dark figure which was holding me down. Many people see these dark shadowy figures, which are usually seen standing by the foot of their beds, or in the corners of their rooms. They are referred to as Shadow People. There are a few standard Shadow People: a tall man wearing a hat, a small boy who plays with something in his hands, a mass in the upper corners of the room, and an old lady. Of course, details of these figures are never seen, just shadows of their figures.

During the same time that I had my Shadow Person experience, I was taking a Fairytale and Folklore English elective in college. I became fascinated with the oral history of fairytales, and from then on decided to research and document local ghost stories because they too were a type of folklore.

Ghost Tours Are Born

I graduated from college, spent eight years as a graphic designer and art director, married my husband, and moved from Los Angeles, California to Bisbee, Arizona. We moved to Bisbee knowing that it would be the perfect place to start a ghost tour after seeing it on an episode of the TV show *Ghost Hunters*. My husband's parents had been living there for almost ten years, and the first time we went to visit them, I knew that I had to move to the quaint town.

It was shortly after the move that I started the Old Bisbee Ghost Tour. I then wanted to share the ghost stories of local neighboring cities and therefore decided to branch out with the Tombstone Ghost Tour and Tucson Ghost Tour. My involvement with the preservation of the ghost stories and the local history lead the local Bisbee Chamber of Commerce to award me the title of Official Ambassador to the Ghosts and Spirits of Bisbee.

As the ghost tours grew, I knew that I needed to become better educated in the paranormal and started to seek out a paranormal investigation group to join. This is how I met Christy Necaise who is the lead investigator and founder of the International Community of Paranormal Investigation and Research, ICPIR for short. ICPIR's professionalism and dedication to the paranormal investigation field won it the 2008 Ten Best Examiner's Award. When the team goes on an investigation, they try to rule out all things explainable that have a human or environmental influence. The ICPIR members use scientific processes and deductive reasoning. They gather research and data through the use of tools such as Digital and Film Cameras, Camcorders, EMF Detectors, Digital and Cassette Recorders, IR Thermometers and Motion Detectors.

Christy and I met in Tombstone, Arizona, one hot afternoon and we hit it off right away. We have been on numerous investigations together since then, including the Western Heritage Museum, Bird Cage Theater, Copper Queen Hotel, and Bisbee Inn.

In this book when we talk about a haunted location, which has been investigated by ICPIR, I will make a special note about it with a description of our experience and findings. It is very interesting to compare and contrast the folklore about haunted locations to the paranormal investigations that have been conducted there.

I am delighted to be writing a book about the ghost stories and folklore of the ghosts of Bisbee, Tombstone, and Tucson, and to preserve their place in history. Some people believe in ghosts, some people don't. The folklore in this book are the stories that have been told to us from the locals who have had the stories passed on to them from the people who experienced them firsthand.

What Are Ghosts?

How can you read a book about ghosts without first understanding what a ghost is and what a haunting is?

When you think of a ghost, your mind probably goes to images of the movies such as the *Exorcist, Blair Witch Project, Ghostbusters* or even *Poltergeist*. The fact is that these are just movies and were made to scare you and put fear into you—they act as entertainment. The reality is that there are no documented cases of anyone ever being killed by a ghost. Though some claim to be hurt by them, those people possessed by spirits will yield scratches and other physical marks on their person. These cases are very rare. Ghosts have received a bad reputation over the years; but please note that most of the time, they are completely harmless. We are scared of them because they are "the unknown." We as mortals do not understand the unknown and that is why we have a fear of it. As we come to understand what ghosts and spirits are, our fears will lessen.

A ghost is defined as being a spirit of a deceased person who shows itself in a human likeness. That is a pretty broad definition! Many people believe that human beings are made up of energy, and that after we die, the energy lives on in the form of ghosts. Ghosts are put into different categories; here are just a few with their definitions. These types of ghosts and hauntings will be referenced within this book.

Intelligent Ghosts/Hauntings
Ghosts or spirits that interact with humans and the space they haunt and are believed to be able to communicate with us in one form or another.

Residual Ghosts/Hauntings
When a ghost is seen doing the same thing, in the same place, over and over again. Think of a tape recorder recording our energy at a specific event or location and then playing it back over and over again.

Object Ghosts/Hauntings
Instead of a building or place being haunted, the ghost connects itself to a specific object. Jewelry, furniture, dolls, old weapons can all be related to Object Ghosts or Object Hauntings.

Poltergeists
A German word, which means "noisy ghost." The ghost will make noises, or throw objects. Many believe that a Poltergeist is not a ghost at all, but an event, which usually surrounds prepubescent adolescents. The theory is that the prepubescent in the household has so much energy stored inside of them that they make objects move without knowing it. It may also occur with adults who are going through very emotional times, such as a divorce, or the loss of a loved one.

Shadow Ghosts or Shadow People
Shadow-like beings that show themselves in photos as dark forms. Usually seen out of the corner of the eye, these beings sometimes take the shape of human forms though have no human features.

Portals
Believed to be a passageway to our dimension that ghosts or spirits use to travel through.

A Brief History of Tucson

Some 12,000 years ago, the first Paleo-Indians roamed what is now Tucson. Evidence of such tribes has been found along the Santa Cruz River. In 1692, the Mission San Xavier del Bac was founded along the Santa Cruz River and this settlement was named Tucson. In March of 1856, the United States captured Tucson from Mexico. It had been a part of Mexico until the point of the Gadsden Purchase. In 1885, after Tucson became the capital of the Confederate Arizona Territory, and after Arizona became part of the New Mexico Territory, the University of Arizona was founded in the city.

After World War 1, many veterans who had been gassed during the war started coming to Tucson because of the dry air that was good for their lungs. Tucson then started development of the Veteran's Hospital. Since then, people have come from all over the world to Tucson because of the clean dry air and warm climate.

In the 1880s the city of Tucson received a very special gift, the Southern Pacific Railroad. In that year, the population of Tucson grew to 8,000. The railroad is what kept this city alive and thriving because it was now connected to the rest of the world. It brought people heading west to California's gold rush. Some of these people stopped in Tucson, seeking to find wealth there. In 1912, Arizona became a state.

Today, Tucson's second biggest employer is the University of Arizona; Davis-Monthan Air Force Base also provides the city with lots of job opportunities. Tourism is another huge industry in Tucson with an estimated 3.5 million visitors a year.

St. Augustine's Cathedral

St. Augustine's Cathedral. The ghost of a woman dressed in black is seen walking in front of the building. *Photo Courtesy of Author.*

Type of Hauntings: Residual

HISTORY

St. Augustine's Cathedral was built as part of the Spanish fort that occupied the area around the corners of Ochoa and Stone Streets. It started out as a one-room building where the priest lived and where soldiers came to pray. Throughout the years, additions were added to the building until its completion in 1868. The original plans showed that the church was to be built in the Gothic style seen throughout Europe, but, lack of funds caused the plans to change. In 1966, the building was deemed unsafe for worshippers and a restoration project began. The restoration continued through the cathedral's 100th birthday celebration.

Many devout Roman Catholics come to St. Augustine's Cathedral to pray and mourn. The cathedral is illuminated at night and is so magnificent that it slows traffic driving by. It can also be seen from the 10 Freeway while traveling through Tucson.

PARANORMAL ACTIVITY

There have been sightings of an apparition of a Hispanic woman dressed in black from head to toe. She is seen walking back and forth in front of the entrance to the Cathedral. She appears both during the day and at night and has been spotted several times by residents of nearby houses as well as by a gentleman who lived in an upstairs apartment on 6th Street.

They describe her as looking sad, with her head lowered, as if she is in mourning. Most state that when they see her, her back is always facing them. She then turns her head around—and only her head. The man who lived in the apartment building was told that for many years nuns lived in the apartments near where he lived, and he thought that she might be a nun who once prayed at St. Augustine Cathedral. He, too, saw the lady in black walking back and forth in front of the cathedral. She never frightened him; though, when he saw her, she always made him feel morose.

Who is this woman dressed in black? Could it be the spirit of a woman who lost her love? Or is it the ghost of a nun who still comes here to pray and to do the Lord's work long after her body has departed this world?

It is a Tucson mystery that may never be solved.

SCOTTISH RITE BUILDING

Scottish Rite Building. Note St. Augustine's Cathedral to the right.
Photo Courtesy of Author.

Type of Hauntings: Residual

HISTORY

The Scottish Rite Building that stands at 160 S. Scott Avenue in downtown Tucson was built in 1915. It is on the National Registry of Historic Places. A Master Mason's education of the first three degrees is carried out by the Masonic organization known as the Scottish Rite. It is part of a worldwide fraternity known as the Freemasons. The Scottish Rite building is where the Freemason's fraternal brotherhood holds their secretive meetings.

Part of the building was closed down after the discovery of several dead bodies. Many believe they were the bodies of transients who were using the basement room as sleeping quarters. That section of the building was closed out of respect for those who passed and because it was old, unsafe, and not being used anymore.

Today, the Freemasons use the building to hold meetings and stage plays for others in their fraternal brotherhood. It holds one of the largest costume departments in the city of Tucson. The building is a labyrinth of rooms, including meeting rooms, a library, makeup room, and an auditorium with a huge backstage area.

PARANORMAL ACTIVITY

Late at night, janitors who have been working in the historic building have seen glowing apparitions. The most frequent one is seen down the hallway that leads to the back stage area of the Red Room. It is seen by the memoriam of old stage crewmembers. The memoriam has photos of the crewmembers with their personal hats hanging next to their photos.

When the ghostly apparition is seen, they say it looks like a glowing light in the shape of a male human body. It will glow so brightly that it lights up the entire hallway. As the mortals who walk to it get closer and closer, the glow of the apparition gets dimmer and dimmer, until it will eventually disappear. Perhaps the deceased stage crewmembers had such a deep connection with their personal belongings that they now decide to stay with those hanging in the memoriam.

Another glowing apparition is seen in the hallway that leads to the library. Some believe this ghost is that of George Roskruge. George Roskruge was a prime mover for the Masonry in the area who arrived in 1874 from Cornwall, England. He was a member of the True and Faithful Lodge of Helston, England. Could he have loved his fraternal brotherhood so much that his spirit chose not to leave? Or maybe his spirit is looking over his fraternal followers who have come to follow in his footsteps.

The two-headed eagle which is part of the Scottish Rite logo means: "Whom virtue unites death can not separate." The men who are members here believe that the ghosts that haunt their beloved building are all positive spirits. They do not believe that they are there to do any harm. They feel that the spirits were most likely Freemasons who had passed on, but do not wish to leave their cherished friends behind.

SANTA RITA HOTEL

The Santa Rita Hotel as it stood in 2009.
Photo Courtesy of Author

Type of Hauntings: Residual

HISTORY

Built in 1904, the Santa Rita Hotel stood at the center of Tucson's El Presidio district at 88 East Broadway Boulevard. It stood as one of the most elegant hotels in its time. It was built on the former sight of Camp Tucson, which was used after the Civil War to return law and order to the city. It was considered the most posh hotel because it had a roof garden, dance hall, modern plumbing, bathrooms, electricity, an elevator, and telephones. Guests would walk through huge arches to enter the lobby that welcomed them in with the finest furnishings and fixtures.

Unfortunately, the Santa Rita Hotel was closed and has been for some time. As I was writing this book, I was informed by one of our Ghost Hosts on our Tucson Ghost Tour, that the Santa Rita Hotel was scheduled to be imploded. Most likely by the time this book is published the hotel will no longer be standing. An office building with shops and restaurants on the ground floor is planned to replace the hotel. Let's hope that the ghosts who haunt the Santa Rita choose to stay and haunt the future office building as well.

PARANORMAL ACTIVITY

Room 822 was the most haunted room in the building, and oddly enough, it was not always a room. In the 1980s the hotel added the eighth floor. Originally, Room 822 used to be part of the elevator shaft. The ghost who haunted Room 822 was apparently a gentleman by the name of John Ferguson. According to local folklore, Mr. Ferguson was an obsessive compulsive whose wife had an affair, and she became pregnant by her lover.

John was so enraged that he killed his wife, and then hung himself in the elevator shaft, which was later turned into part of Room 822. A terrible desire to clean, as if the obsessive compulsiveness of John Ferguson transferred into their own bodies, would overcome people who stayed in the room. Guests also claim that the TV would go on and off, the bathroom door would open and close throughout the night, and that the lights would go on and off.

Another ghost was seen in the room as well, and it is that of a woman. She was usually seen hovering near the ceiling and then glided gracefully down to the floor to disappear. Perhaps it was Mrs. Ferguson's ghost making her presence known to the guests who have stayed there.

Another spirit, which was believed to haunt the halls of the deserted Santa Rita Hotel, was that of a little boy. The story goes that the little boy was running alongside the pool, when he slipped and fell into the water. He did not know how to swim and he drowned. His ghost is said to haunt the building in search of his mother.

TUCSON RAILROAD DEPOT & TRANSPORTATION MUSEUM

Wyatt Earp and Doc Holliday statue in back of the Tucson Railroad Depot and Transportation Museum. The exact spot in this location where they shot and killed Frank Stirwell is unknown. *Photo Courtesy of Author.*

Type of Hauntings: Residual, Intelligent

HISTORY

It was at this location where Wyatt Earp found and killed one of the McLaury gang members, Frank Stilwell, after they killed his brother, Morgan Earp, in Tombstone, Arizona.

In 1998, the City of Tucson restored the former Southern Pacific Railroad Depot and added three adjacent buildings in the 1941 architectural style. For some reason, the ghosts liked to haunt the old Garcia's Restaurant that stood here long ago but has since been closed due to renovations. In the basement of the old train depot was the jail where they would put prisoners while they awaited their transfer to other cities.

PARANORMAL ACTIVITY

Some believe it is the ghost of Frank Stilwell that haunts this location. Unseen hands move objects and full-body apparitions have been seen. Many have smelled unusual odors near what used to be the restaurant. Strange noises are heard as well. In the Transportation Museum, doors have been known to slam shut by themselves. A museum director, has smelled strange perfume while alone in one of the bathrooms. She thought that smelling such a strange perfume while alone in the building was weird enough; but, when it started to follow her from the bathroom to her desk, it was too strange to discredit. A volunteer at the museum who claims to be a bit of a medium, told the director one day that she sensed a couple spirits in the building. One such spirit was a woman who wore a Victorian-styled black dress. This ghost must have experienced a great loss because she seemed very sad. Yet she enjoyed the director's company and the volunteer said that the spirit would follow her around the building, as well as watch her work at her desk.

PIONEER INTERNATIONAL HOTEL

The Pioneer International Hotel is now an office building in the middle of Tucson's downtown district. *Photo Courtesy of Author.*

Types of Hauntings: Residual

HISTORY

The Pioneer International Hotel located at 100 N. Stone Avenue was built in 1929 and was a thriving twelve-story, sixty-five-room hotel until the dreadful day of December 20th, 1970. On that date, a sixteen-year-old arsonist, Louis C. Taylor, who was a four-time parolee, set fire to the hotel during the Hughes Aircraft Christmas party that was taking place in the ballroom. The fire was set on the sixth floor, and quickly moved up through staircases and hallways, trapping many people in their rooms with no way out except to jump from windows.

The fire department stated that if there were doors between the stairways and hallways, the fire would have been contained. Instead, it used the stairways as a path to go higher and higher into the top floors of the building. There were no fire alarms, smoke detectors, or sprinkler systems in the building. Had these safety features been present, the fire would have been extinguished before any lives were lost. The Tucson Fire Department's trucks were not equipped to handle a sky rise building fire. Their ladders only went as high as the fifth and sixth floors. Guests staying on the upper floors started jumping out of the building to escape the fire and smoke. Twenty-seven people were injured and twenty-eight people died. Most of the deaths were due to smoke inhalation.

One woman jumped out of a seventh-floor window to her death. Others died from their burns, while some succumbed to carbon monoxide poisoning. Killed in the fire was Harold Steinfeld who was the builder of the hotel and the owner of a department store located across the street from the building. His wife died next to him in their penthouse apartment.

Taylor was found guilty of starting the fire and was sentenced to life in prison. The acting detective on the scene said that he felt Taylor started the fire to cause a distraction so he could burglarize some of the hotel rooms.

The Hotel was rebuilt and turned into office spaces. There is a little coffee shop and a flower shop on the ground level where the lobby of the hotel used to be.

PARANORMAL ACTIVITY

The new building is your typical office building and you would not be able to sense its tragic past by just walking through its doors. Mundane gray carpets and white painted hallways make this building seem almost unremarkable, until you start discussing the paranormal activity which takes place in those hallways and corridors.

Most believe that the unfortunate souls who perished during the 1970 fire haunt the building, especially its upper floors. The lower floors get a lot of activity as well. Tucson folklore states that the second floor was used as the morgue during the fire. The acting detective that night was able to debunk this claim. Nonetheless, the second floor does get a lot of paranormal activity. Sounds of people running up and down the hallways screaming are often heard in offices on the second floor. Strangely, the sounds seem to be coming from above them. Upon further investigation by people who work there, there is no one acting in such a way on the third floor.

Those who work on the top floors state that, late at night, people working in the building will hear what sounds like people running around on the upper floors while the building is nearly empty. Smoke has also been smelled near the upper floors though smoke detectors do not go off.

Most of the employees who work there won't comment on the paranormal activity out of respect for those who tragically lost their lives. Though one secretary told us, that her co-workers, as well as herself, would leave no later then 6 p.m. and that most of their contractors will never be in the building after dark for fear of encountering some of the spirits.

Could the Pioneer International Hotel be haunted with residual haunting? Could the ghosts be reliving that fateful night over and over again? One would hope not.

FOX THEATER

The beautiful Fox Theater has some spirits who just don't want to leave. *Photo Courtesy of Author.*

Types of Hauntings: Residual, Intelligent

HISTORY

Construction began on what was to be called the Tower Theater at Congress and Stone Streets on August 24, 1929. By September 1929, the Fox West Coast Theater chain had acquired the property and the Tower became the Fox. Originally budgeted at $200,000, the theater would eventually cost $300,000, including furnishings. Designed as a dual vaudeville/movie house, the Fox featured a stage, full fly-loft, and dressing rooms beneath the stage. The combined effects of "talkies" and the Depression limited the opportunities for live performance, and the dressing rooms were never completed.

On its opening night, Congress Street was closed and waxed for dancing. Four live bands were hired, a live radio broadcast and free trolley rides downtown were just some of the features to celebrate the grand opening.

In 1974, the Fox Theater closed due to competition from television. The vanishing retail and housing of downtown Tucson also contributed to its demise. In 1999, the Fox Tucson Theater Foundation was formed, with the sole purpose of bringing the theater back to the city.

The building was finally refurbished and now the beautiful theater house stands in full operation on 17 West Congress Street.

PARANORMAL ACTIVITY

The ghost of a man dressed in the style of the Depression era is said to haunt the outside of the fully restored theater. He begs for money to feed his family. Perhaps it is the spirit of man who died poor and homeless on the streets of Tucson.

A ghost of a man similar in description is seen inside the theater, walking the backstage area. The projection room is a favorite spot for the ghost or ghosts to haunt. One projectionist was in the projection room, when he noticed a ball of tape on the table moving by itself. The employee asked out loud, "If you're going to play with it, then really play with it." The ball of tape then rolled from one side of the table to the other by unseen hands. The equipment in the projection room had also been disturbed in the middle of the night. Once the projectionist came to work in the morning and the lens on the projector had become unscrewed. To do this, one must use a tool.

The ghosts are benign and very friendly, never causing harm to anyone; they have been said to be more of a nuisance then anything else.

Looking out the window in one of the upper floor windows is the spirit of a gentleman watching the busy street below. *Photo Courtesy of Author.*

HOTEL CONGRESS

Types of Hauntings: Residual, Intelligent

HISTORY

To serve the growing cattle industry and railroad passengers of the Southern Pacific Line, the Hotel Congress was built in 1919. This historic hotel had been the hub of Tucson history and nightlife for nearly a century. Guests not only stayed there for a night or two, but many people have lived there over the years, as the hotel used to rent its rooms month to month. The hotel's Tap Room had been open since the 1930s, and the Club Congress, open since 1985, is one of the most hopping nightclubs in Tucson.

It is intentional that the hotel does not have a TV in any of its forty rooms. The hotel tries to keep its original ambiance. Original amenities were attempted to be preserved, from the iron bed to the vintage radio, the comforting rumble of the nearby iron horse to the retro-style phone that actually connects to a switchboard at the front desk.

John Dillinger and his gang came to Tucson to hide after a series of successful bank robberies. The gang stayed at the Hotel Congress on the third floor under false names. After a fire was discovered in the basement, an evacuation of the building took place. Two members of the gang asked two firemen to retrieve their luggage from their room. It was later discovered that the bags contained a small arsenal and $23,816 in cash. Later, the fireman recognized the gang in *True Detective* magazine. A stakeout took place and they were captured at a house on North Second Avenue. It only took the Tucson Police five hours to catch the gang and they did it without firing a single shot.

The top floors of the building were demolished a few years later and the room that the Dillinger gang occupied no longer exists.

PARANORMAL ACTIVITY

The ghost of a man, who is said to have died of a heart attack in the building, is seen peering out of one of the windows on the second floor of the hotel. Hotel employees refer to him as T.S. and he is usually seen wearing a gray suit. Some dispute that he did not die of a heart attack, but was in fact killed by gunfire over a card game.

An apparition of a beautiful female ghost is seen on the staircase. She is seen wearing Victorian clothing and always has the scent of roses around her. She is more often smelled than seen. The manager has smelled her on the staircase a couple of times. She states that the smell of the roses will only last a couple of seconds, but that it is very distinct, and you know when you smell it that the female ghost is near. Many believe that she is a residual haunting, making her grand entrance to the lobby from the staircase.

In the mid-nineties, in Room 242, a tragedy occurred when a distraught woman took her own life by shooting herself in the head while sitting on the toilet in the bathroom.

She is said to haunt the room to this day. People staying there often hear her talking to them as they sleep or feel her sit on the bed next to them. Guests who have never met her and sleep in the room will dream of this woman, often having nightmares. A full apparition of her is often seen outside Room 242, in the hallway. The hotel tried to cover the bullet hole that went from the bathroom into the closet, but there is still evidence of it if you know where to look.

On this staircase many have seen the ghost of a woman. She smells of roses. *Photo Courtesy of Author.*

Vince is a gentleman who lived at the hotel for thirty-six years. He would use the butter knives from the Cup Café as screwdrivers when he needed to fix something in his room or in the hotel. Current staff members have claimed to find these butter knives all over the hotel hallways. They believe that Vince is still with them and still has a fondness for his butter knife repair kit.

The maintenance man has seen the apparition of a cowboy in the basement. The man was going into the basement's paint room to pick up some paint for a project he was working on. He opened the door and saw the ghost of a cowboy standing in front of him, but he only saw this ghost from the waist up. The maintenance man was in such a rush, he walked through the ghost who was standing there, got what he needed, then walked out of the room. It all happened within a few seconds. It was not until moments later that he realized that he had walked through a spirit entity.

A gentleman was staying at the Hotel Congress and his window was open. A gust of wind woke him and his dog. The dog barked endlessly at the bathroom. After calming down the dog, the gentlemen went back to sleep. When he awoke the next morning, he found all the towels, which were neatly placed on the towel racks, stuffed into the toilet. We are unsure which ghost at the hotel would have done such a thing, but perhaps it was one who did not like the dog barking at him.

ROYAL ELIZABETH
Bed &Breakfast

The paranormal activity occurs in the rooms which are located on all sides of the main entrance way. *Photo Courtesy of Author.*

Type of Hauntings: Residual, Intelligent

HISTORY

When you walk through the doors of the Royal Elizabeth B&B you expect to see Norma Desmond relaxing on one of the sofas in the parlor reading a magazine. The inside of this hidden treasure is filled with antiques, has stained glass skylights and seventeen-foot-high ceilings. Between its construction and the present, the house has only had five owners. Charles Rivers Drake, who was a prominent figure in Tucson in the late 1800s, originally built the house. He was in the Army and was stationed at Fort Lowell, which is now Armory Park located across the street from the B&B. While in the Arizona Territory he met the love of his life, Agripine Moreno, and in 1872, they were wed.

Agripine came from a very prominent family in Sonora, Mexico. She was very assertive, self confident, and strong willed. A couple of years after retiring from the army, Drake built the house that is now the Royal Elizabeth B&B. The house is built in the San Francisco Victorian Style and is the only one of this style made of adobe.

All who met him during his life liked Drake because he was of fine moral character. He worked hard and was honest in his work and money. In 1888, Agripine died in the house that she shared with her husband and numerous children.

PARANORMAL ACTIVITY

The owners of the house have told us that they have at least three ghosts that haunt their lovely home. One of these is believed to be that of Agripine Moreno. The ghost likes to provoke aggressive, self-assertive women who are staying alone at the Royal Elizabeth. One guest was staying in the Rose Room and woke up to a female ghost with its hand on her cheek holding her down, not in a mean way, but in an authoritative way.

Multiple guests staying in the Rose Room have seen the ghosts of three children coming out of the bathroom and running across the bed, through the door, and into the parlor.

The second owners of the house were the Blenman Family.

Mr. Blenman built a safe room under the house during the Indian War. The entrance to this safe room was through the floor of the Rose Room. It is believed that the Blenman children would play in the safe room while their parents were not around. We therefore believe that the ghosts of the children coming out of the bathroom in the Rose Room are the residual haunting of the Blenman children coming out of their secret playing spot.

The spirits here like the owners to pay attention to them. It is not uncommon for the owners to be alone in the house, and while cleaning up, have lights, fans, and faucets going on and off. In the Purple Room, towels on the towel rack have fallen onto the floor. In the Blue Room, after cleaning the room, the sink faucet was turned on by itself. The owner turned it off and went about his normal daily activities only to find that the faucet was running again. So he turned it off again. This continued many times during the day. One day all the lights in all the guest rooms went on by themselves, and the owners had to go into each room and turn them off. Guests have stated that in the middle of the night, lights and fans have gone on by themselves.

The Purple Room has a side door that opens out into the garden area. Almost daily the door will be latched shut and then mysteriously open by itself. The owners state that when in the pool area, they will look over at the door and it will open ever so slowly and remain open until one of them closes it. The owner's dog, Lucy, that has since passed away, was once in the garden area and kept sticking her head through the fence to the pool, wagging her tail and acting ever so happy. She then moved down the fence as if she was following someone who had just given her praise or petted her head. A guest had once seen the apparition of a ghost walking the same pathway by the pool that Lucy the dog walked.

THE MANNING HOUSE
Type of Hauntings:
Residual, Intelligent

HISTORY
Levi Howell Manning came to Tucson in 1884, at the age of twenty. He quickly realized that money could be made in the

electricity industry. He became the General Manager of the Ice and Electric Company. He sold his interest in the company and from it accumulated a small fortune. From that fortune he built the Santa Rita Hotel, and helped bring the trolley to Tucson. In 1905, he was elected the Mayor of Tucson and served until 1907.

It was in 1907 that Manning started to build the Manning House on ten acres of desert property. The grounds were always kept green with lush grass, trees, and flowers. The original house was 12,000 square feet and combined the Spanish Colonial and Santa Fe Territorial styles. It had just enough room for the Manning Family that consisted of his wife, Gussie, her four children from a previous marriage, their son, and Gussie's granddaughter.

Manning died in 1935. Since his death, there have been many renovations made to the house by his children and grandchildren.

In 1949, the family decided to move and they sold the house to the Elk's Lodge. The Elk's Lodge added many of the renovations that now make the Manning House 36,000 square feet.

Today, the Concannon Family of Tucson owns the Manning House and they rent out the facilities for banquets, weddings, proms and concerts.

PARANORMAL ACTIVITY

It is believed that the original owner, Levi Howell Manning, haunts the mansion which he built and raised his family in. Guests and employees have seen the ghost of Manning pacing up and down the hallways with a candlestick. Guests of the house have seen the apparitions of a young girl and a gentleman leisurely walking in front of the building. The current owners, as well as many employees, have heard unexplained noises. Kitchen appliances have turned on and off by unseen hands, as well as the kitchen faucet. Numerous psychics have also felt the presence of the ghost of a little girl in the kitchen. One guest of a party that was taking place in the house had to use the restroom to freshen up. While looking at her reflection in the mirror, she saw a floating face behind her. This guest got so scared she vowed never to return to the Manning House.

Tombstone

A Brief History of Tombstone

In 1877, Ed Schieffelin came to the Arizona Territory in search for a mining miracle, and he found it! Silver, and lots of it! A friend of Schieffelin told him that all he would find in the Wild West would be his tombstone, and thus Schieffelin decided to name his claim "The Tombstone." In 1879, the town of Tombstone was founded and named after Schieffelin's famous claim.

The population of Tombstone in 1881 was 1,000 people; by the next year, the population rose to an estimated 10,000 people. The county seat was in Tombstone and it was considered the biggest town in Cochise County at the time. There were no railroads to get to and from Tombstone, and the outlying areas were vast and deadly, with uncivilized men calling themselves Cowboys and the dreadful Apache Indians.

On October 26th, 1881, the famous Gunfight at the OK Corral occurred. This fight was the result of a long feud between some of the Cowboys and the Earp family. They disagreed on business practices, law, and politics. The Earps had come to Tombstone to find their riches in the silver mines, and also to uphold the law and justice in town. During the fight at the OK Corral, thirty shots were fired in thirty seconds. Three of the Cowboys were killed, the McLaury Brothers and Billy Clanton. Morgan Earp, Virgil Earp, and Doc Holliday were injured while Wyatt Earp walked away unharmed.

Because of Tombstone's location in the middle of the desert, water was scarce and a company came in and built a pipeline to supply the town with water. A little while later the silver mines started to flood with water. A pump was installed to pump the water out. Soon after, the pump started to fail, and Tombstone soon became a ghost town. Many of the miners headed thirty miles west to Bisbee, where the mines were still active. The county seat was moved to Bisbee a few years later and Tombstone fell into ruins.

It was not until the mid 1960s that a group by the name of the Historic Tombstone Adventurers came to the once-booming mining town and refurbished some of the old buildings. These structures, which were no longer buildings, but just wooden shells, were just a hint of what Tombstone use to be.

Today, Tombstone, Arizona, gets an average of 400,000 tourists a year, most of whom grew up hearing stories, watching movies and TV shows about the Wild West town, and want to see it for themselves. The town's main industry is tourism, which is apparent when walking down Allen Street. Though most of the buildings are not original, the ones that line the boardwalk today are replicas of those that stood there over 100 years ago.

THE OK CORRAL

Where the gunfight at the OK Corral took place, the middle of Fremont Avenue.
Photo Courtesy of Author.

Types of Hauntings: Residual

HISTORY

The back of the OK Corral is where the most famous gunfight in U.S. Southwest history took place. Most believe it occurred behind the walls of the current establishment, which states that it is the OK Corral. It has shows throughout the day reenacting the gunfight, but in fact most of the fight occurred on Fremont Street, behind the OK Corral. Three men were killed during the gunfight, Tom and Frank McLaury and Billy Clanton. Tombstone folklore says that after Tom McLaury was shot, he crawled down the street and died in agony shortly thereafter, wrapped around a post that stood on the street corner, where a telephone pole now stands. A bullet grazed Doc Holliday. Morgan Earp was shot in the shoulder. Virgil Earp was shot in the leg and Wyatt Earp left the scene unscathed.

PARANORMAL ACTIVITY

People have claimed to see a floating glowing ball of light at the famous site. Some have heard voices and footsteps when no one was around. One of the managers has seen a full apparition of a tall thin gentleman wearing a brimmed hat. A ghost with a beard has also been seen peering through the windows of the building.

Could these ghosts be that of the McLaury brothers or Billy Clanton staying here to seek their revenge on the Earps some 125 years later?

GHOST TOUR

On the opening night of our Tombstone Ghost Tour, a strange photograph was taken. A woman took a photo of the historical plaque outside the OK Corral on Fremont Street. These types of plaques are positioned throughout Tombstone and mark the location of historic events. When she showed the photos to the tour guests later in the night, everyone agreed that what they saw in the photograph was a face. The face is described as that of a young man about thirty years old, with a moustache, hat, and a very stern, almost angry expression in his eyes. The local town historian was asked about this photo. He explained that many people have seen this young male ghost on Fremont Street, behind the OK Corral, where the photo was taken. Most people who have seen this ghost believe it is the ghost of Tom McLaury, waiting around to take his revenge on the men who killed him.

THE HISTORIC TOMBSTONE COURTHOUSE

The Tombstone Courthouse is the smallest state park in Arizona.
Photo Courtesy of Author.

Types of Hauntings Residual

HISTORY

Housed in the smallest State Park in Arizona is the Historic Tombstone Courthouse. Built in the Victorian Style and shaped to symbolize the Roman Cross, this Courthouse was built in 1882, during Tombstone's short-lived mining boom. With the population of Tombstone growing, Cochise County was established, and the new county needed a new courthouse and county seat. So the Cochise County Courthouse was built in 1882 and at the time cost $50,000. The Courthouse became home to the local sheriff, recorder, treasurer, jail, board of supervisors, and the gallows in the back where condemned prisoners were hung.

After the silver mines in Tombstone closed, and Tombstone's population started dwindling, the county seat was moved to Bisbee. In 1931, the last office in the Courthouse was closed.

The building remained vacant until 1955. In 1959, it was taken over by the Tombstone Restoration Commission. They refurbished it and turned it into a historical museum and a national park where guests can wander the halls and learn the history of Tombstone.

PARANORMAL ACTIVITY

Late at night, if you watch the tower at the top of the Courthouse, sometimes you can see shadows of people walking back and forth. This is a very common occurrence, though no one knows who these shadows belong to, for they are seen long after the park closes for the night. Many believe that the shadows are the ghosts of the men who were hung on the gallows. Also heard are frightened ghostly screams coming from the back of the building. It is no coincidence that in the back is where the gallows once were, and where they have been currently reconstructed for the public to see. This is where public hangings took place. Perhaps the screams heard are those of the relatives of those men who were hung here over a hundred years ago. Or perhaps it's the screams of the dead whose spirits are stuck in the national historic park for eternity.

Schieffelin Hall, where Morgan Earp was seeing a show on the night he was killed. *Photo Courtesy of Author.*

SCHIEFFELIN HALL
Types of Hauntings:
Residual, Intelligent

HISTORY

Schieffelin Hall, located on Fremont Street, is the biggest adobe building in the U.S. Southwest. When Tombstone was a booming silver town, Schieffelin Hall was the only respectable theater in town. It was where the most lavish of shows, the greatest of operas, and the best vaudeville performances were held. At that time, Tombstone was considered one of the best Theater Towns around. Schieffelin Hall was built in 1881 by the brother of Tombstone's founder, Al Schieffelin and William Harwood. Besides seating 600 people during its lavish theatrical performances, the building was home to the King Solomon Masonic Lodge. The night of March 18th, 1882, Morgan Earp was shot and killed. Earlier in the evening Morgan and his brother Wyatt saw a show at Schieffelin Hall.

Once "talkies" came, the theater moved with the times and started showing moving pictures. After the mines flooded, and everyone left town, Schieffelin Hall fell into a state of disrepair, being used only by the Masonic Lodge. In 1963, the Historic Tombstone Adventurers bought the building, restored it, and then donated it to the city. In 1966, it was placed on the National Register of Historic Places.

It is now used as the local Justice Court and is where City Council meetings are held. The theater is still operational, and from time to time, local theater groups hold performances there.

The stage inside Schieffelin Hall where some paranormal activity takes place.
Photo Courtesy of Author.

PARANORMAL ACTIVITY

The ghosts that haunt Schieffelin Hall do not suffer from stage fright. They enjoy haunting the dressing room while actors are getting ready for performances. Noises are heard when no one is there. The Woman in Red is a prominent ghost in the dressing room. She is believed to have been an actress that performed often in the theater and has even been seen by one of our Tombstone Ghost Tour's Ghost Hosts.

While investigating the ghost stories, the guide went backstage and down the stairs to the dressing room. The lights were not on in the dressing room. When the guide looked in the floor length mirror, she saw looking back at her, the reflection of the Woman in Red. The Women in Red was wearing a long red evening dress with a large brimmed red hat. By the time the guide called to the City Clerk who was giving her the tour of the building, the Woman in Red was gone.

Most of the paranormal activity occurs when preparations are being made for a performance on this historic stage. The ghostly spirits must enjoy the new shows that entertain them, though they are the ones who provide the thespians with entertainment of the scary type. Props have been known to go missing or to be moved. The piano can be heard playing by itself and spurs can be heard walking around the entrance hall when no one is there.

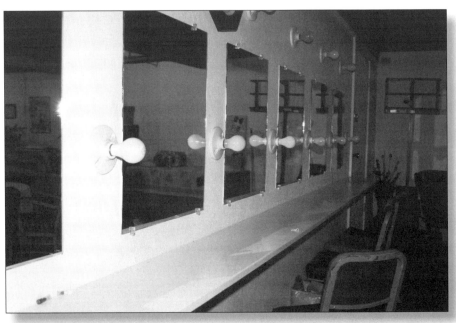

The dressing room where most of the paranormal activity takes place. This is also where one of our Ghost Hosts saw the Lady in Red. *Photo Courtesy of Author.*

The City Clerk has heard a loud and deep exhale coming from behind her when she was the only person in the building. Doors she would keep open overnight would close and lock by themselves. The ghosts do not like her electronic equipment and sometimes in the morning when she comes in, the printer and fax machine won't be working and she knows that the ghosts have been fiddling with them, trying to figure out what the equipment is and what it does.

BELLA UNION BUILDING

The Bella Union Building where our Tombstone Ghost Tour Ghost Hosts can watch objects move week by week through its windows. *Photo Courtesy of Author.*

Types of Hauntings: Residual, Intelligent, Object

HISTORY

The Bella Union Building, built in the early 1880s housed the town's U.S. Post Office. Tombstone folklore states that the building's second owner was from China and turned the building into one of the seediest opium dens in Tombstone. It didn't last very long, as the story goes, because one evening, while high on opium, the owner and another drugged gentleman thought it would be a good idea to have a knife throwing contest. The gentleman threw a knife, missed his mark but instead impaled the owner in the chest, who died shortly thereafter.

The building now houses a bar and restaurant, which has not been open in years. Dust resides on the tables and floors. Bottles of liquor stand abandoned as one peers into the uncovered windows of this once nightspot turned vacant building. Perhaps the current owners feel that the ghosts who haunt their building might scare away patrons.

PARANORMAL ACTIVITY

Most of the locals believe that the ghost of the Chinese owner has never left the building. He liked to play little tricks on the patrons when the establishment was open to the public, such as unraveling an entire roll of toilet paper, making the silverware on tables shake and move about, starting the dish washer and coffee maker, opening and closing doors, turning on and off lights, changing the radio station, and lighting candles.

Several locals have reported a more polite side to the spirit as well. They each told of using the restroom when the building was open, only to discover upon sitting down that the stall was out of toilet paper. As they each considered their plight a roll came over from the next stall. The relieved patrons would pick up the roll and thank the occupant of the next stall. When they didn't receive a response each of them reported bending down to look into the next stall; they discovered that the stall was vacant.

The previous owner, who lived in an apartment attached to the back of the building, woke up one morning to find his home ransacked. After surveying the damage, he checked all the doors and windows, which were all locked and latched from the inside. He closed the establishment shortly thereafter.

There is a large fabric doll that sits above the bar with a reputation for movement. Many guests on the Tombstone Ghost Tour have noticed the doll kick her feet and hitch herself up, or follow them by turning her head.

There is also an apparition that is seen walking down the staircase to the left of the Fremont Street entrance. Most of the time, all that is seen is the ghost from the waist down. The door at the top of the stairs has also been known to open and close by itself on many occasions and additionally, the door will open and close gradually over weeks or months.

Other objects in the building seem to move as well. In the dining room, there is a gambling table where the dust on the table shows that cards and poker chips have been rearranged. In another section of the building there resides an antique piano that often shows finger marks in the dust. Beyond the piano is another door that opens and closes on its own.

Can you spot the doll that witnesses claim moves by itself? *Photo Courtesy of Author.*

CORNER OF 1ST and TOUGHNUT

The Bisbee Mob lynched John Heith; it is the only lynching that ever took place in Tombstone. *Photo courtesy of the Bisbee Mining and Historical Museum.*

Type of Hauntings: Residual, Intelligent

HISTORY

John Heith is the only person who has ever been lynched in Tombstone, Arizona. The story though begins in Bisbee, Arizona, a mere thirty miles away. Bisbee was also a booming mining town, and Heith opened a saloon there, which was a known hangout for the local outlaws.

On December 8th, 1883, five men, Daniel Dowd, Comer W. Sample, Daniel Kelly, William Delaney and James Howard held up the Goldwater & Castenada Store on Main Street in Bisbee. They were told that the payroll money for the Copper Queen Mine was held in their safe. Two of the men went inside, and to their surprise, the safe had less then half of the $7,000 they presumed would be there. The men inside then decided to rob the customers and employees of any money or valuables they had. The other three men were keeping watch outside. They started to get impatient because the robbery was taking so long and started shooting at anyone they could. They shot a man by the name of Tappenier through a window. A Deputy Sheriff, Tom Smith, rushing to investigate the shooting in the street, was immediately shot. A pregnant woman by the name of Annie Roberts was also shot. A gentleman named Nolly was killed while standing outside his office. The entire shooting spree took place in less then five minutes, and the outlaws left town and never looked back.

Bisbee's Sheriff immediately notified Tombstone Sheriff Ward about the incident. Ward's response was to form two posses, one lead by himself, the other by Sheriff Daniels. Daniels came to Bisbee to interview witnesses.

John Heith's saloon was down the street from where the shooting took place, so Daniels questioned Heith on what happened. Heith told Ward that he knew the men involved, since they were customers of his saloon, and then proceeded to tell Ward which direction they were headed. Sheriff Ward, knowing that Heith was involved with a bad crowd, knew not to trust him. Soon enough Sheriff Ward figured out that Heith had lead them off the real trail of the suspects and onto a fake one to throw the law off their tracks.

Eventually, the posses found and caught the five men. After they were questioned, it appeared that Heith knew more about the robbery than originally thought. Some of the men involved told the Sheriff that Heith planned the entire thing.

All five men were tried, on February 17th. They were found guilty and sentenced to hang on March 8th, 1884.

Heith was arrested as well, but was given a separate trial. He stated during his trial that he was the mastermind behind the robbery; but he never intended for anyone to be killed. He claimed it was not his fault that the lookouts started shooting. He also stated that when he started to hear gunshots, he got so frightened, that he dropped to the ground and hid behind the bar of his saloon. Heith was convicted of second-degree murder and conspiracy to commit robbery. He was sentenced to a life sentence at Yuma Prison, though he never made it there.

On the morning of February 22nd, a mob of Bisbee citizens went to the Tombstone Jail and broke Heith out. They were extremely upset over the sentence he received and wanted vigilante justice. On a telegraph pole, at the corners of 1st and Toughnut Street, they hung a noose and lifted Heith's protesting body up and up until it dangled limp and deceased, high above the estimated fifty-man mob.

The other five men involved were hung on March 8th and then buried in Tombstone's Boot Hill Cemetery alongside their friend John Heith.

PARANORMAL ACTIVITY

Residents near the intersection of 1st and Toughnut have repeatedly heard what sounds like a mob of people outside. They claim to hear screams, yells and protest sounds, as if crowds of people

1st and Toughnut as it looks today. *Photo Courtesy of Author.*

are right outside their windows; yet when they go to see what is going on, the streets are vacant. This ruckus happens at all times of the day and night with no logical explanation.

Many who live around that famous intersection believe that the ghostly voices they hear are from the Bisbee Mob who hung Heith, and of the protesting screams of Heith himself as the mob hung him from the telegraph pole.

BIG NOSE KATE'S

Big Nose Kate's is a popular spot to get a bite to eat, hear some local music, and see a ghost. *Photo Courtesy of Author.*

Types of Hauntings: Intelligent, Residual

HISTORY

When you walk through the typical bar swinging doors of Big Nose Kate's, you are immediately transported back in time. The saloon gives you the feel of the Wild West. The former Grand Hotel of Tombstone housed Wyatt and his lawful wife, Mattie, when they first arrived in Tombstone. It is now Big Nose Kate's, a saloon and dining hall named after Doc Holliday's on again, off again girlfriend, Kate. Kate was a woman of negotiable affection, and though she never owned this building, it was named after her since she was such an infamous figure of the Wild West.

When this building was The Grand Hotel, it had a janitor who lived in the basement. After he finished his duties, he would go into his basement bedroom, away from the hustle and bustle of the world above him. It was in this dark basement retreat where he started digging for silver. He dug himself a mine and Tombstone folklore states that he found plenty of silver in his secret mine. He is believed to have hid his silver fortune somewhere in the Grand Hotel, safe from the greedy hands of those who would want to steal it if word got out about his secret treasure trove. Before the janitor could sell the silver, and spend the money, he passed away.

If you choose to go into the basement of Big Nose Kate's, you can still see "The Swamper's" sleeping quarters and the entrance to the mine where he found his precious silver.

PARANORMAL ACTIVITY

To this day, the ghost of this janitor is said to haunt what is now Big Nose Kate's. The legend says that his ghost is trying to protect his silver and to keep people from finding it. The employees here have named the ghost, "The Swamper." After closing, some have seen him late at night sweeping the floors.

The basement is now a gift shop. Employees have seen clothes being thrown from the walls onto the floor by The Swamper. Female employees have been pushed while walking down the spiral staircase leading to the basement. Mannequins, located above the bar, have been pushed from above onto the floor below. The Swamper likes to play with the lights on the spiral staircase going from the dining hall to his secret mine, too.

The Swamper is not the only ghost that haunts The Grand Hotel. Above the bar, in what used to be the second floor of the hotel, is where the women of the evening carried out their business. When the room is still and you listen very carefully, you can hear the ghost ladies walking around in their high-heeled boots, pacing as they wait for their gentlemen callers to pay them a visit.

The Swamper's sleeping accommodations which is where he accessed his secret mine. It can still be seen if you go into the basement of Big Nose Kate's. *Photo Courtesy of Author.*

GHOST TOUR

While I was attending the Tombstone Ghost Tour, to observe how the tour was progressing, our Ghost Host needed some water to clear the dust out of her throat. The closest establishment was Big Nose Kate's. I decided to venture in, despite the huge amount of tourists and bikers, who were getting ready for their night on the town. I flagged down the bartender and asked her for a couple bottles of water. Before she went to the other side of the bar to get the bottles of water, she placed two steins under the beer taps and allowed them to fill up. As she was walking back to my end of the bar with the bottles of water in hand, the two steins, now filled to the top with beer, came out from the beer dispenser towards me, floated in mid air for several seconds, and then crashed to the floor. I started laughing with excitement, because this was the first personal experience I had ever witnessed in Big Nose Kate's. The bartender was not as amused. I paid for the waters, tipped her well and went back to rejoin the Tombstone Ghost Tour to share my experience.

During another tour, several young women had already told the guide that they had visited Big Nose Kate's earlier in they day and had encountered some trouble in the basement gift shop. After the guide had described the Swamper's fondness for making messes, the women started laughing. When asked why, they told the group that when they had been in the gift shop that morning, every time they picked something up to take a closer look at it, a mess ensued. When one of them was removing a shirt from a rack, the entire rack collapsed. They then moved on to check out a display of mugs. As soon as they touched a mug the rest of the display fell over. They had several other such experiences before giving up, worried that they were going to damage something beyond fixing and be forced to buy half the store's merchandise. After describing the incident they laughed and told the group that they were glad to know they Swamper has a fondness for such tricks, as they claimed to not be as clumsy as their experience would indicate.

CORNER OF 5ᵀᴴ and ALLEN

Known as one of the bloodiest intersections in the United States. *Photo Courtesy of Author.*

Types of Hauntings: Residual

HISTORY

The intersection of 5th and Allen is where Virgil Earp was shot and crippled. Sixteen other men were not as lucky as Virgil, and left their bodies in the dust here during Tombstone's wild years. On three of the four corners were bars and saloons. When you mix booze and guns, the results are not those that most would desire.

PARANORMAL ACTIVITY

The ghosts of those who have died at this intersection can be seen on the nights of a full moon. Some see the ghost of a little girl walking up Allen Street. Every ten to fifteen feet, she bends over and picks up a ghostly object from the ground. Many believe she is picking up flowers, yet there would not have been flowers growing on Allen Street. Some believe that she lived on a street that had flowers, and for some reason she is lost and thinks Allen Street is where she used to live. Others feel that she is not picking up flowers at all, but rather money on the ground.

There is a man often seen at this intersection. He wears a Victorian suit and a bowler hat. Many say that he is walking to the Bird Cage Theatre. It must have been one of his favorite places to drink and gamble.

A Tombstone local told a lady who lives in nearby Sierra Vista, that to see a ghost in Tombstone, you have to come to Allen Street during a full moon in the wee hours of the morning. She and a few friends decided to give it a try. Dressed in their pajamas at 3 a.m., they came to Allen Street to see if they could spot any of the famous ghosts that haunt it. To their surprise, soon after their arrival, they saw the apparition of a gentleman dressed in a camel-colored duster and matching cowboy hat, with spurs on his boots. He had dark hair and a mustache. The gentleman was walking up the street, checking to make sure all the business' doors were locked tight. LeeAnn and her friends observed him checking on at least four doors before they decided to walk towards the ghostly figure. As they did, he crossed the street diagonally away from them, disappearing into thin air.

CHARLESTON ROAD

Could the spirit of one of the deceased buried in the cemetery be haunting Charleston Road? *Photo Courtesy of Author.*

Type of Haunting: Intelligent

HISTORY

There are lots of urban legends in the United States about hitchhiking ghosts that haunt vacant streets. Most of these stories take place on streets near cemeteries. The folklore usually states that a woman will be walking down the street, someone will pick her up in a car, and the woman will indicate that she lives near a cemetery. Of course, by the time the driver gets to the location where the woman has said she lived, she has disappeared into thin air. Tombstone is no exception to this urban legend. Many of these hitchhiking ghosts are seen on the old road that leads from Tombstone to Sierra Vista. It is called Charleston Road. Being very hilly, Charleston Road is the scene of many car accidents. The road is so curvy and tricky that if a driver is not paying attention, it is easy to drive off the road. There have also been many reports of suicides off the Charleston Bridge that goes over the San Pedro River.

PARANORMAL ACTIVITY

In May of 2002, a gentleman who used to work with my husband, his wife, their three children, and sister-in-law had just finished a shopping trip to Walmart in Sierra Vista. They were in their 2002 Jeep Cherokee Laredo driving back to Tombstone down Charleston Road. They stopped at a red light across from the local DMV office. As the light turned green, the man started to drive and then noticed a woman on the right hand side of the road. She was walking in the same direction they were driving. She was Native American, had long, black straight hair and was wearing blue Levi jeans, a white top, and white shoes. The driver could not control the urge to pull over and ask this woman if she needed a ride. He rolled down the window, leaned over his wife who was in the passenger seat, and asked the stranger if she needed a ride anywhere. She responded, "Yes I do."

Two of the children moved into the back of the jeep, with the bags from Walmart, to make room for their traveling guest in the back seat. The son, who was on the passenger side in the back seat, moved over closer to one of his sisters who was now sitting behind him. The stranger got into the back seat of the car with the daughter and son. After she closed the door, the man continued to drive down Charleston Road. At the next light, which was less then a mile from where they'd picked up the mysterious woman, she told them that this was where she was going and to let her out.

They pulled over at the Sierra Vista Cemetery and the woman got out of the car, closing the door behind her. The driver rolled down the window to wish her well, and noticed that she had disappeared.

Everyone in the car started looking for her, but she was nowhere to be seen. The man even got out of the car and circled it in a state of confusion wondering what happened to the woman who only moments ago was sitting in the back seat of his car. Finally, he got back into the car and started whispering to his wife so as to not frighten the children about what had just happened.

His son, from the back seat, kept trying to interrupt the adult's confused conversation. They were in a state of shock, when after a couple attempts he was able to get his parent's attention and stated, "That woman was ice cold when she was sitting next to me."

They will never forget that day on Charleston Road and the mystery of who this woman was will remain in their minds for eternity.

If anyone else other then my husband's friend had told me this story, I might not have believed them; but, coming from such an honest, trustworthy gentleman, who not only worked with my husband, but was a City Councilman, I have no choice but to trust every word he said. He stated that if I didn't believe his story that I could call everyone who was in the car that day and they would have recounted the same event.

AZTEC HOUSE

The abandoned Aztec House. *Photo Courtesy of Author.*

Type of Hauntings: Residual

HISTORY

The Aztec House was built in 1880, but vacant by 1889. It was considered an upscale and high-rent boarding house for men only. Some of the witnesses of the "Shootout at the OK Corral" were residing at the Aztec House. It was located right across the street from where the shootout took place. Women of negotiable affection, bought by men staying there, were allowed in the building. After servicing the men, they were usually thrown out onto the street. One of the Madams of these women protested the poor treatment that her girls received at the house. She quickly was accused of running an illegal prostitution ring. The men accusing her felt that a woman of such ill repute should be killed, and so it is believed that they carried out her brutal murder.

PARANORMAL ACTIVITY

The Madam, who is also referred to in Tombstone as the Lady in White, is seen walking up and down Fremont Street outside the Aztec House. She has been known to stop traffic on the major street when drivers think that she is a real human, wandering around in the middle of what is also known as Route 80. Sometimes she is seen crying, but always wearing a white floor-length gown, with her white hair done up in a fancy bun.

Some say that the ghost of a woman whose child died of Yellow Fever is also known to haunt the building—not wanting to leave her deceased child behind.

Many females who enter the building encounter paranormal activity, from hearing voices, to getting their hair pulled. Some feel that the more angry or hostile the women who enter are, the angrier and more hostile the ghosts will react to them. The spirit has been known to make women physically ill, and to cause such discomfort that they need to vacate the premises. Though many well-mannered women, who are respectful and polite, seem to have no negative effects from the ghosts or hauntings in the building.

THE BUFORD HOUSE

The Buford house is believed to be haunted by a few spirits. *Photo Courtesy of Author.*

Types of Hauntings: Residual, Intelligent

HISTORY

George Buford lived in the house that he built in the late 1880s with his father. It's situated on a quiet street off of the busy bustling Allen Street. The house is a very ordinary two-story home.

The urban legend in Tombstone states that George Daws lived in the Buford House and fell madly in love with his neighbor across the street, Cleopatra Edmonds. There was no work for George in Tombstone, so he moved to Bisbee to find work in one of the mines. He returned nine months later after saving all his money, ready to marry his Cleopatra. After returning home, George, Cleopatra, and a group of friends went out for a night on the town. By the end of the evening, Cleopatra decided that she no longer loved George, and instead went home with one of the male companions who accompanied them that evening. George was enraged and the next morning took a gun, crossed the street, and shot Cleopatra four times; he then returned home and turned the gun onto himself, which resulted in his suicide. Cleopatra though did not die; she survived her assault and lived on for fifty more years.

The Buford House was used as a Bed and Breakfast for many years until closing down and becoming a private residence.

> This is a private residence. If you choose to visit, please observe from the street and do not disturb the current owners.

PARANORMAL ACTIVITY

From the outside, this building does not appear to be haunted, though once you walk inside, the chills may cover your body from head to toe. In fact, it was so haunted that it was featured on the History Channel's "Haunted Histories" show.

Of course, people assume that the ghost of George Daws, the ill-fated lover, haunts this building. His ghost has been known to turn lights off and on, ring the doorbell, to turn faucets on and off, knock on doors and windows, as well as stroke women's hair. His full-body apparition has been seen strolling after dark in front of the house. Guests staying at the house have been jolted awake and then had their covers thrown across the room. Others have heard their names being called when they were alone in the house.

There is also believed to be the ghost of an elderly woman that haunts the premises. One guest claimed to have seen this apparition sitting in a rocking chair in one of the rooms. It screamed at her, "This is my room, get out!" When this elderly lady's ghost is near, some say they can smell her perfume.

WESTERN HERITAGE MUSEUM

Western Heritage Museum is filled with real artifacts from the Wild West of the 1800s to today. *Photo Courtesy of Author.*

Types of Hauntings: Object, Residual, Intelligent

HISTORY

The original building was built in 1880 and was the home of the Herring Family. Sara Herring, who was raised in the house, was the first female attorney in the state of Arizona. Her father, Colonel Herring, moved out west to settle the estate of his deceased brother. He caught the mining bug and decided to stay to find his fortune. Unfortunately, he was a better lawyer than miner. Though to the Earps, this was very fortunate, for Colonel Herring was Wyatt Earp's attorney during the murder trial following the shootout at the OK Corral. Wyatt Earp was ultimately acquitted of all charges regarding the crime. In 1896, the family moved out of Tombstone to Tucson where they practiced law.

Then, 105 years later, the building was turned into one of the finest museums of Tombstone's history. The museum has one of the rarest Tombstone photos known to exist. It is a photo taken by C.F. Fly of the Clantons and McLaurys. It is the only known photo of Billy Clanton taken while he was alive.

The museum also has on display:

- Allie and Virgil Earps' drop leaf table that they purchased in Tombstone,
- the original hand written license that opened the Bird Cage Theater dated December 24th, 1881,
- the *Tombstone Epitaph* newspaper from the date of the OK Corral shootout and on the date of the McLaury's and Clanton's funeral.

The museum has a gift shop as well. Off the gift shop are the living quarters where the owners live.

HAUNTINGS

The female owner is the one who has experienced most of the paranormal activity. One of the spirits she has is named Mary. She does not know why she calls her Mary, but feels that this is her name. When sitting on the back patio, with the door is open, you can see all the way through the house. In the evenings, when they first moved into house, they would sit on the back patio and would see a mist floating through the house portion of the building.

One time, when they were going from the house to the shop, she saw, out of the corner of her eye, a woman. The woman was gone by the time she turned her head and she was unable to get a description of what she looked like, only that she was a female.

The kitchen in the house is entered from the living room. There is a door that separates the two rooms. One night, while sitting in the living room, the owner heard someone walk into the kitchen. Thinking it was her husband, she wondered why she didn't see him walk past her to get to the kitchen. These footsteps and sounds are those you would normally associate with the activities of a kitchen. Curious to see what was happening, and confused that she did not see her husband walk past, the owner walked into kitchen. Her husband was not there. At the same time she entered the room, all the noise stopped. Throughout the years, they have heard walking footsteps, creaking boards, and tapping sounds, yet when they try to follow the noises, no one is there.

One of the spirits seems to be attached to some of the items in the museum, particularly the guns that the spirit's father is believed to have made in the 1880s. They believe her name is Minni. She has a distinct perfume that has a rich violet smell. The fragrance of her perfume is often contained to a small area and then disappears.

Another one of the spirits once locked the owner in the hallway. All the doors around her were locked, and she started to get nervous and scared. She verbally spoke out loud and told the entity to "let her out." All of a sudden one of the doors opened all by itself.

A friend of the owners was staying in the guest room off of the museum. While there, their friend saw a full-body apparition of a man wearing a long trench coat walk across the hallway. While in the shop, she heard noises coming from the museum. She looked into the museum area and saw a dark figure. Knowing that no one had been in the museum the entire day, she rushed in, walked down every aisle, and looked behind every nook and cranny. No one was there.

While they were working on the museum one day, the owner decided to leave her keys in the door to make it easier for her to get in and out without having to ruffle through her pockets for the keys every time. She was leaving the museum and was about to reach out to turn the keys, when she noticed that they were swaying in the door. A gentleman who was working for her told her that he hadn't come through the door for ten minutes. The keys kept swinging for at least five minutes without stopping.

GHOST HUNT

In April of 2008, I went on my first Paranormal Investigation with the International Community of Paranormal Investigation and Research. The investigation just happened to be at the Tombstone Western Heritage Museum. Christy was doing the Preliminary Investigation as Kevin and I set up some of the equipment. After we set up the cameras and other equipment, we strategically placed glow sticks around the building so that we would have an easier time getting around the floor plan. No flash photography was allowed due to the artifacts in the museum. We went lights out and started the investigation, I was nervous, scared, excited, and could not wait for a paranormal experience... though one must always be careful for what they wish for.

Our main focus during the investigation was in the museum area of the building, though there were a few rooms off the shop that were known to have activity as well. Being that this was my first investigation, I decided to stay close to the other investigators and mostly observe what was going on. However, they threw me right in and I immediately started doing EVP work with Kevin.

Out of the corner of my eye, I kept seeing a dark shadow moving around two mannequins in the museum. One mannequin was wearing authentic clothing from the 1880s; the other wearing a replica of 1880s attire. Also seen during the night were shadows walking past the door.

We went outside to try to recreate the shadow figure and were unable to do so. While Kevin was walking up and down the aisles doing his own EVP work, I sat down near the counter where I could watch the museum area for anything paranormal. While Kevin walked up the aisle where the mannequins were, he asked a question, and all of a sudden one of the glow sticks we had placed on a piece of wood flew across the aisle right behind him. We caught it on film, which was really beneficial to us.

There was one room, off the hallway near the shop, in which many of the investigators began to experience a creepy feeling. Kevin and I decided to do some EVP work in that room. The room was filled with boxes and shelves and no bigger then seven feet by seven feet—there was very little room to move. One of my hands held the digital recorder; the other I had placed on my hip, with my elbow pointing out. We started asking questions and nothing was happening. Then all of a sudden I felt a touch on my elbow. I looked and saw no one standing there. I very calmly turned to Kevin and said, "I think something just touched my arm." I knew that I was not allowed to freak out or go screaming out of the building, but that is exactly what I wanted to do. I knew that there was no physical being in the room with us; yet, I also knew that something had touched me and I didn't know why. It is the most memorable experience I have ever had on an investigation, and I'm sure will remain so.

MILTON HOUSE

The Milton House is being restored to its original beauty, hence why some of the paranormal activity is being stirred up. *Photo Courtesy of Author.*

Type of Hauntings: Residual

HISTORY

Jefferson Milton made history by being the first Immigration Border Patrolman. He spent his life working in law enforcement including being the chief of police in El Paso, Texas, a Deputy U.S. Marshall, and eventually, in 1904, joining the Immigration Service. Milton lived in Tombstone for a short period of time from the 1930s to the early 1940s after he retired from law enforcement.

The Milton House, as it is called, was the home that he shared with his wife, Mildred. Located on 3rd Street, this house was originally built by William Gird, whose brother was one of Tombstone's founding fathers. The house was two separate homes put together to make one larger home. Today, it is being restored and the owners are planning to open it as a museum in the near future.

PARANORMAL ACTIVITY

Since the beginning of the renovations, much paranormal activity has occurred in this historic home. The owners have seen unexplainable lights and shadows, and they have heard voices. A stack of neatly piled papers on a table one moment was a neatly stacked pile of papers on the floor the next. The owners were unable to recreate this strange occurrence. A tenant in the back living quarters saw a glass of water slide on his kitchen table for a distance of two feet, with no explanation of how it slid across the table or why. A friend of the owners was at the house and saw a man by the front door. When he went to answer the door, no one was there. Dark shadows seen one minute and gone the next are not uncommon. One evening, when a friend was visiting, the owner saw a dark shadow move across the room. He thought it was his friend, and when he followed the shadow, he realized that his friend was at the opposite side of the house. They tried to recreate the shadow and were unable to do so. The spirit of a male ghost wearing a black vest with a white shirt and hat has been seen walking through the kitchen of the building. The presence of a female ghost has been seen dressed in black walking from room to room of the home.

The reason these ghosts are so active now, and have never been mentioned before the new owners took over the house, is probably due to the renovations. A common theory is that any new construction to a haunted building will cause the ghosts to act up. It is believed that the construction confuses the spirits and causes them to be more active.

Who the spirits are is an entirely different question, and one which we do not have the answer for. Since the house is over 100 years old, and has had numerous owners, it is safe to say that a couple of them were fond enough of the building to not want to leave.

BRUNCKOW'S CABIN
Type of Hauntings: Residual, Intelligent, Shadow Ghost

HISTORY

Off Charleston Road, between Tombstone and Sierra Vista, you will find what used to be the Brunckow Cabin. Frederick Brunckow was a Prussian-born miner who came to Arizona to find his claim. He struck silver and started mining near the San Pedro River. Building a cabin near the river in the 1850s, he lived there along with his Mexican workers. In those days, Arizona was a very dangerous place to be. It was unsettled and not yet a state. Arizona was riddled with Apache Indians who would not hesitate to kill anyone found trespassing on their land.

It is believed that Mexicans, wanting to take the silver ore that Brunckow found, killed Fredrick Brunckow in 1860. They put an end to him by taking his rock drill and drilling it through his body. They then threw his body down his own mineshaft. A total of twenty-one deaths have taken place at the cabin. Thus, it was nicknamed the bloodiest cabin in Arizona.

After Brunckow's death, it is believed that Ed Schieffelin used the cabin for shelter, and he used the fireplace to smelt his ore.

Today it is abandoned and only ruins remain. Unfortunately, vandals and souvenir hunters have destroyed most of the cabin. The cabin is located on private property, and due to the vandalism, it is strictly off limits. Please view the cabin from the road.

PARANORMAL ACTIVITY

In 1891, a Tucson newspaper first made claims that the cabin and mine were haunted. Many who try to camp and spend the night at the abandoned adobe structure seem to be scared away by unseen hands touching them and moans and groans coming from the old mine shaft where Brunckow's body still remains. Many have seen and photographed shadowy figures walking the grounds of the old cabin. Some claim to hear the sound of a flute being played, as it is known that Brunckow liked classical music and would bring in flute players to play for him. The sounds of dragging bodies are heard as well as screams and the sound of people running. Cold unseen hands have touched people and many experience a feeling of uneasiness when around the mineshaft and ruined cabin.

RED BUFFALO TRADING COMPANY

Red Buffalo's Trading Company was the building where Morgan Earp was shot by an unseen assailant. *Photo Courtesy of Author.*

Type of Hauntings: Intelligent

HISTORY

Red Buffalo Trading Company used to be the Campbell & Hatch's Saloon and Billiard during the years that the Earps were in Tombstone. It was in this saloon on March 18th, 1882, that Morgan Earp was shot by an unknown assailant. The bullet is believed to have come from the back window. He died in the building, on one of the pool tables.

PARANORMAL ACTIVITY

Employees working here today say that a ghost haunts them on a daily basis. Female employees have been pushed over. Boxes that have not yet been emptied and sorted move to different spots all over the store by themselves during the night when the store is vacant. Employees have come in the morning to find all the fan pulls on the floor for no apparent reason. Most assume the culprit is the ghost of Morgan Earp.

CRYSTAL PALACE

There have been grown men who have come running out of the Crystal Palace scared due to the ghostly activity. *Photo Courtesy of Author.*

Type of Hauntings: Intelligent, Residual

HISTORY

The Crystal Palace used to be the Golden Eagle Brewery but was destroyed in the fire of 1882. In July of that year, the Crystal Palace was built. The downstairs of the Palace was one of the more upscale bars in town. The management made an effort to keep the riff raff out. The upstairs housed offices. The office of Virgil Earp who was then the U.S. Deputy Marshall was on the second floor, as well as the doctor who announced the deaths of the McLaury Brothers and William Clanton after the gunfight at the OK Corral.

Prohibition closed the Crystal Palace during the Depression. Between then and the 1960s, it has been a movie theater, a Greyhound Bus station, restaurant, and curio shop. In 1963, the Historic Tombstone Adventurers renovated the Crystal Palace to its original beauty. The bar inside is not the original bar. The original bar was moved to a cantina in Mexico that has since burned down. The current bar is a replica that was duplicated by using old photographs taken inside the original Crystal Palace.

PARANORMAL ACTIVITY

The ghosts that haunt the Crystal Palace act as though the doors have never closed. Since the Crystal Palace was one of Big Nose Kate's favorite hang outs, it is not surprising that she has been seen walking around the main floor. Her ghost is seen along with the ghosts of cowboys waiting at the bar for their next drink. The roulette wheels on the wall start spinning and making noise all by themselves and many believe that the ghosts of the gamblers who used to hang out here spin them in hopes of winning one more game. The lights will turn on and off by themselves, and objects will move when no one is around. Bartenders closing at night will hear footsteps and voices in the unoccupied bar as well as a grandfather clock chime—yet there is no grandfather clock in the building. There is also a ghost that likes to hang out behind the bar and has been known to put his hands on female bartenders while they are tending bar. Though never violent, he disturbs the bartenders and makes sure that they know they are never alone.

BIRD CAGE THEATRE

The Birdcage Theatre believed to be one of the most haunted buildings in the American southwest. *Photo Courtesy of Author.*

Type of Hauntings: Intelligent, Residual, Shadow Ghost

HISTORY

One of the most haunted places in America is the Bird Cage Theatre. The theater opened in 1881, and was very famous in its day for being the ultimate honky tonk. It used to be open 24 hours a day, 7 days a week, to entertain the men who came here to drink, gamble, see the cancan show, or to be entertained by the ladies of negotiable affection in the fourteen cribs which hung above the dance floor. The proper women of Tombstone never dared to enter or even come near the Bird Cage Theatre.

It was at the Bird Cage that the world's longest poker game in Western history occurred. Players had to buy a minimum of $1,000 in chips to have a seat at the game table. It ran continually for 8 years, 5 months and 3 days. The original bar is still there, and is the only original bar from any building in Tombstone. There are 140 bullet holes in the ceiling and walls of the Bird Cage from the 16 gunfights that occurred there. When the mines started to flood in 1889, the Bird Cage closed and was locked up tight with all its fixtures, and red velvet curtains were sealed behind the doors. It remained that way until 1934, when it was reopened to the public and became a Historic Landmark of the American West.

There is a famous urban legend about two women who lived in Tombstone. One was named Gold Dollar and the other one was named Margarita. They were both in love with the same man who went by the name of Billy. Margarita was extremely attractive and spent her days and nights at the Bird Cage Theatre flirting with the men, and allowing them to buy her drinks. She set her sights on one man in particular, Billy, who happened to be Gold Dollar's boyfriend. While Gold Dollar worked down the street at the Crystal Palace, Margarita and Billy could be found at the Bird Cage Theatre drinking, dancing, and embracing each other in a manner inappropriate for public viewing. One evening while Gold Dollar was at work, a patron approached her and informed her that he had just seen Billy and Margarita in the Bird Cage. Gold Dollar left the Crystal Palace and started screaming in the streets, "I'm going to cut her heart out!" as she rushed over to the Bird Cage. She got there just in time to see Margarita sitting on Billy's lap kissing him passionately. She watched them for a short period of time before she approached them. She took out a knife that was hidden in her garter, which she carried for protection against men who tried to go too far with her at the Crystal Palace. In her jealous rage she walked over to the couple, knife in hand, and plunged the knife deep into Margarita's chest. She died on the spot. No one really knows what happened to Billy and Gold Dollar after that tragic event at the Bird Cage Theatre.

When you walk through the doors of the Bird Cage Theatre, on your left you see the original bar and back bar, on your right you see an original painting gifted to the establishment by one of its favorite performers. After you enter the museum, authentic pieces of Tombstone's past surround you. As you look up you see the cribs, still framed with their red velvet curtains. Tables along the walls and in the middle of the room display original antiques from Tombstone's heyday. As you look straight ahead, you see

The stage where a man has been seen walking from one side to the other.
Photo Courtesy of Author.

the stage where the performances were held. Below the stage is a piano that was used to play music to entertain the patrons. As you walk behind the stage, the Black Mariah, the original horse drawn hearse that took the dead to their final resting place at Boot Hill Cemetery, draws all the attention. Along the walls are photos of women who are believed to have performed at the theatre. To the right of the Black Mariah, is a long creaky staircase going down to the bordellos. It is in the basement room where the longest poker game took place. The bordellos are furnished with antiques and clothing, as if the ladies of negotiable affection went out for a Sunday stroll only never to return. You exit the Bird Cage through a gift shop where books and souvenirs are waiting for you.

PARANORMAL ACTIVITY

The ghosts that haunt the Bird Cage Theatre act as though the theater never closed down. Many who visit, or work there have seen apparitions of those who wish not to depart from their beloved honky tonk. It is not uncommon to see the ghosts of women and men in period clothing walk across the stage, or to hear laughing and music playing after closing, or before opening. Many have smelled the cigar smoke and the alcoholic beverages of the spirits of gamblers who have never left. Some see an apparition of a woman dressed in all-white period clothing, wearing a hat or bonnet, walk from the back stage area down the stairs to where the poker room and private cribs used to be located. This might be the same lady of the evening who is heard singing a sad song from the cribs on the second floor. The sounds of spurs are also not an uncommon occurrence from within the walls of the Bird Cage. There have been many photographs taken of the Black Mariah, the original Boot Hill horse-drawn hearse, which is permanently on display in the backstage area of the Bird Cage. In the photos, you can make out faces of people who lived long ago peering into the hearse. Patrons have reported seeing the large leather bag displayed on a shelf above the Black Mariah start to shake. When they report

The Black Moriah was the original Boot Hill Hearse. Many see faces peering back at them when gazing into the hearse. *Photo Courtesy of Author.*

it to the staff on duty that the Doctor's Bag, as they typically refer to it, is shaking, the staff chuckle and inform the guests that the bag is actually the Undertaker's bag full of tools.

Then there are the reports from the current employees. One employee was opening up and doing her morning walk through. As she was looking at the hearse, she saw two men peering back at her through the opposite window. She said they were both wearing white shirts and black jackets. Both men wore mustaches.

The same former employee was working the front desk when she saw a man on the catwalk. She described him as having a mustache, a receding hairline, and dark eyes. She made eye contact with him and he then immediately ducked down. She could no longer see him. Thinking it was someone who snuck inside the building, she went to the catwalk to catch him and throw him out. When she got onto the catwalk and made it half way to the wall where the man was seen, she suddenly got chills over her entire body. She could not move. It was at that moment that she realized that the man she saw was really a ghost.

A male employee was once grabbed on the shoulder and then slammed into the bookshelf in the lobby area. He has heard female voices whispering his name and saying "Good Morning" to him when no one was in the building. He also had a ghost tug on his hair. He once came by the theater at 11 a.m. to check how business was doing. When he peered into the window, he saw a woman standing behind the front desk where no one except employees are allowed to be. He said that she was dressed in a white dress and she had blond hair that was all done up. He came inside the building and the lady had disappeared. He asked the woman working the front desk who that lady in the white dress was, and the front desk employee replied, "What lady? There hasn't been anyone here in two hours."

There is a video camera system hooked up all over the building, and one of the monitors is in the gift shop. The same gentleman employee who saw the ghost dressed in white, was working in the gift shop, he peered over at the monitor and saw a nude woman walk across the stage to the card table, and then disappear into thin air.

A visitor came to tour the Bird Cage and shared her paranormal experience in the theater. She was walking towards the back part of the Bird Cage; she heard country music softly pouring out of a speaker overhead and paused to listen. At that moment, she felt her neck prickle and then she heard a woman's voice whisper in her ear, "I don't like this music." The voice then began singing an old song from the 1800s. The tourist glanced around to see where the voice came from, but she was the only one in the room at the time. The woman does not limit her criticism to the music. She has been captured via Electronic Voice Phenomenon describing a young gentleman in great and none too polite detail.

There seems to be yet another spirit who enjoys communicating with the staff through one of the speakers located in the lobby of the building. Several sensitives have given his name as Jake, and the spirit seems to enjoy being referred to as such. The spirit will make his presence known by causing the speaker mounted on the right side of the catwalk to hiss with static. This has been known to happen at various times throughout the day rather than at regular times. Usually the noise only lasts for a few moments, but he has been known to make longer statements.

On a paranormal investigation of the Bird Cage sponsored by the Tombstone Ghost Tour and ICPIR, several of the investigators began to discuss a woman who had often performed at the Bird

The wine cellar where a gentleman took a photo of a ghost on his cell phone camera. *Photo Courtesy of Author.*

Cage. The speakers began to hiss in response. The investigators raised their voices and the speaker's hiss increased in volume in response. The investigators stopped talking and the hiss quickly died. Notably the speakers had all been unplugged prior to the investigation to prevent any such interference.

The wine cellar is in the basement of the theater; this is also where the poker room and private cribs are located. A gentleman was taking a photograph of the wine cellar with his cell phone camera. He finished and was looking through them when he noticed, in one of the photos, there was a man sitting in the wine cellar. The man in the photograph was dressed in denim pants, a denim shirt, and a brown cowboy hat. He was sitting in a crouching position by the last barrel. The man who took the photo ran into the gift shop and showed an employee the photo. Together they went back to the wine cellar. No one was there. She said that there would not have been any way for a grown man to even get into the wine cellar, being that the only entrance was locked and no one working that day had access to the key.

On any given day you can take a tour of the Bird Cage Theater and experience some of the ghostly phenomenon for yourself. Photos are often taken of orbs, faces, and ghostly objects in the Bird Cage Theater. At this time, every Wednesday through Saturday night, they host their own ghost tour where guests are given a close-up peek of where the spirits have been seen, heard, and smelled, and then they sit everyone down at a table in the backstage area and turn off the lights for twenty minutes for a truly chilling experience. A great deal of activity has been reported during these "lights-out" periods. Guests have heard pebbles falling on the stage and have collected them afterward. One guest felt an odd tug on his breast pocket, and when the lights came back on he put his hand into the pocket and much to his surprise found a shiny new 1950 Wheatback Penny. A variety of EVPs have been captured, and several female guests and staff have reported feeling hands gently caressing their backs and throats.

GHOST HUNT

In July of 2008, the Old Bisbee Ghost Tour and Tombstone Ghost Tour held their first Paranormal and Ghost Hunting Weekend. The weekend consisted of a Paranormal Investigation lecture by Christy from the International Community of Paranormal

One of the bordello rooms. Can you see a figure of a woman wearing a shawl over her head in the mirror? *Photo Courtesy of Author.*

Investigation and Research followed by a Ghost Hunt of the Bisbee Inn/Hotel LaMore in Bisbee, and a Paranormal Investigation of the Bird Cage Theatre in Tombstone.

We arrived in Tombstone at 6 p.m. while dark storm clouds were forming in the distance. The weather report called for summer thunder and lightning storms. This did not damper our spirits because, when there are thunderstorms, it is believed to heighten the paranormal activity. We split the group into smaller groups of ten people. They each had an hour inside the Bird Cage, with the lights off and the IR cameras rolling. They were free to wander the building trying to find the spirits that are believed to haunt it. Members of ICPIR were strategically placed throughout the building.

The first group went in, and as they made their way through the Bird Cage, little was happening. Donovan from K101 Radio in nearby Sierra Vista was on hand with his high-tech audio recorder trying to catch EVPs during the investigation. He was in the poker room by himself, and started to get scared and uncomfortable. It was very strange for Donovan to react this way, so some of the investigators and guests went into the poker room to see if any of their equipment would go off, or if any photographs could be taken of an unseen entity. Almost immediately after going into the poker room, the women in the group started to get touched, some got poked lightly, others had experienced slight tugs on their hair.

When I followed them into the room, I started to get a bad headache in the back of my head. When I moved next to one of the male investigators from ICPIR the pain in my head would go away. When I was not next to a male, it came right back. This went on for the duration of the evening. When the females in the groups entered the room, the activity was heightened. When they left, it stopped.

One of the guests who was a little psychic stated that there was a male entity standing underneath the staircase. The conclusion we came up with was that there was a male spirit in the poker room in the Bird Cage Theatre. We believe that he did not like the females in the group to be in the room with him because we were supposed to be either performing for him, or "entertaining" him in one way or another. He did not want the females there with him, though he did not mind the males. They were supposed to be there, playing poker, drinking, smoking and being "entertained" by the women as well.

Another one of the Bordello Rooms. Why does it look like there are finger marks in the dust on the mirror, where as the rest of the dust on the dresser seems untouched? *Photo Courtesy of Author.*

My headaches have come back while on other investigations. It is my own "Ghost Meter." I can tell if a presence is close by my headache and the intensity of the pain. I guess, during this Bird Cage Investigation, I was able to tune into unknown psychic abilities I never knew I possessed.

The cages where men could watch the show below and be entertained by a woman of negotiable affection at the same time. *Photo Courtesy of Author.*

Opposite page:
A photo taken outside the Birdcage Theatre on the Tombstone Ghost Tour. We believe the dark mass is one of the ghosts who haunts the building. Many people have caught on film black masses in and around the old honky tonk. *Photo Courtesy of Author.*

Bisbee

A haunted staircase in the Bisbee Inn/Hotel Lamore. *Photo Courtesy of Author.*

A Brief History of Bisbee

Bisbee was founded in 1880 and was named after Judge Bisbee, who was one of the financial backers of the Copper Queen Mine. Silver, gold, and copper were found in the hills now known as Bisbee. The land was so rich in minerals that Bisbee exploded in popularity during the late 1800s, when miners and immigrants seeking work came west. Over three million ounces of gold and eight billion pounds of copper were brought out of the mines there. In the early 1900s, Bisbee was the largest city between the Mississippi River and San Francisco. Its population grew to over 20,000 and was considered the most cultured city in the Southwest. Bisbee is home to Arizona's first public library and the oldest continuously active baseball field, as well as the state's first golf course.

However, it had its rough side, too. Within the city limits there were over 100 bars and brothels. In 1908, a fire destroyed most of Main Street, but it did not destroy Bisbee's spirit. Businesses and homeowners rebuilt. These rebuilt structures are what you see today if you take a stroll down the Main Street of this National Historic Landmark. In the mid 1970s the mining operations ceased as it started to become unprofitable to continue mining. This is when all the miners left, and the artists and hippies moved in, purchasing their homes from anywhere between $100 and $5,000. Today, Bisbee is an eclectic artist's community and tourist destination.

BISBEE GRAND HOTEL

The Grand Hotel's bar where lots of paranormal activity occurs after hours.
Photo Courtesy of Author.

Type of Hauntings: Residual, Intelligent, Object

HISTORY

Located at 61 Main Street is the Old West Victorian-styled building, The Bisbee Grand Hotel. It consists of six suites, each with its own theme, and seven guest rooms.

It was built as a hotel for the mining executives. When the fire of 1908 occurred, all the businesses from the Fire Station, which is now the Bank of America building, all the way up Main Street to Castle Rock, including The Bisbee Grand Hotel, burned to the ground. The Grand was rebuilt using cement and brick instead of wood, and was constructed more extravagantly than it had originally been. In the reconstruction, a saloon with a bar top from the Pony Saloon in Tombstone was added.

PARANORMAL ACTIVITY

Not only did the living guests return to the Bisbee Grand, but the dead ones did as well. The Bisbee Grand Hotel is the only hotel in Bisbee where there are stories of patrons running out of their rooms in the wee hours of the morning with nothing but their pajamas due to the paranormal activity.

In the 1980s, the hotel was renovated to the glorious piece of work that it is today. During the renovations, guests were not allowed into the hotel; so, it was odd when one of the construction workers saw a lady walk up the staircase and into the Victorian Suite. He followed her to explain that the hotel was not open for business and that guests were not allowed inside. When he walked into the suite, she had disappeared into thin air. He described the Lady he saw to the owners, and they confirmed that he had seen their Lady Ghost.

The Lady Ghost has been known to peer over people while they are sleeping, so the guests will wake up to her looking down upon them. She also enjoys tugging on guests' ankles while they sleep. She will open and close doors and turn the lights on and off. She has also been known to take the fresh towels, neatly arranged by the housekeeping staff, and put them in a pile in the middle of the floor.

The story of the Lady Ghost is a tale of Bisbee folklore. When Bisbee was a booming mining town, there was a preacher who would visit annually on his route through mining towns in the American Southwest. His wife died and he took on a companion to keep him company. While in Bisbee, he stayed at the Grand Hotel. It was here where he passed away in his sleep. His companion lived on, and after she died, her ghost is said to have come back to the Grand Hotel in search of the preacher. She was his companion even in death. No reports of the preacher's ghost have ever been reported at the Grand Hotel.

The bed in the Oriental Suite is believed to be haunted. The story I've heard about the bed is that it is a Traditional Chinese Wedding Bed, given to a bride and groom on their wedding day. It was in this bed where they consummated their marriage. Shortly after the wedding night, the bride died. The bed was sold at an auction where the Bisbee Grand Hotel purchased it. Guests who have stayed in the Oriental Room have reported the bed to be haunted. Many have experienced the covers and pillows being thrown off of the bed in the middle of the night, and landing in the entry room. Others have reported that the doors and drawers above the head of the bed have opened and closed by themselves seemingly by unseen hands. While guests were in the bathroom, they have seen apparitions of someone walking around and appearing on the bed. Since the hauntings only take place on or around the bed, we believe that this is a perfect example of an Object Haunting. We believe that the ghost of the bride is so attached to the wedding gift that she refuses to leave it, and dislikes when strangers sleep on it.

The saloon has its fair share of paranormal activity as well. The most social of the ghosts is named Jeremiah. Legend says that Jeremiah was cheating at a game of poker. One of his fellow card players figured out he was cheating and shot him in the back of the head. Female customers of the Saloon have seen him in the ladies' room, where he likes to bang on trashcans and stall doors to make his presence known. When not in the bathroom, he likes to haunt the bartenders while they are alone in the bar preparing to close. One bartender saw Jeremiah walk from behind the bar to the fireplace and then disappear. Another bartender had closed up the bar, turned off all the lights and was about to lock up when he remembered that he forgot something. He went back and turned the lights on when a voice from nowhere said to him, "We are closed." He quickly turned the lights back off and left. He quit his bartending job at the saloon the next day.

Another bartender was closing for the evening. She got everyone out of the bar, locked the doors and went to the restroom. All of a sudden the lights turned off. The only way to turn off the lights in the ladies' restroom is by going through two locked doors and pulling a circuit breaker. She left the restroom and decided to clean the glasses behind the bar. She suddenly felt someone massaging her back. She turned around and no one was there.

Another bartender was closing for the evening. He made sure to announce to everyone who teased him about being afraid of closing the bar that evening, that he was not afraid of ghosts, nor did he believe in them. As he closed up, he got everyone out of the bar, locked the doors, and went to use the bathroom. While in the bathroom, he heard his bar full of people having loads of fun, laughing, singing, hooting, and hollering. He thought he might have left the door unlocked by accident and went out to shoo everyone out of the bar. When he walked into the bar, it was completely empty. He decided to sit at a round table at the end of the bar to count out his tips and have a beer to calm down his nerves. He looked up just in time to see a male ghost walk from the mens' room across the hallway to the ladies' room. He described this ghost as a male figure glowing blue. He spilled out the rest of his drink and yelled to the spirit out loud, "I am outta here!"

Jeremiah has also been known to haunt the rooms on the ground level of the hotel. He tugs on women's hair and blows in their ears. He is also believed to leave the Grand Saloon and walk into the shops with shared walls. At the 55 Main Gallery next-door, female employees have felt an eerie presence. They say he just watches them as they close up shop at the end of the day. He always stays in the back area of the store, near the ladies' rest room. Upstairs from 55 Main Gallery, the owner's dog started barking at an unseen spirit, and quickly raced out of the building with his owner in tow on the other end of its leash. To my knowledge, the owner of 55 Main Gallery performed a sage cleansing on her building and told the spirits, whether it was Jeremiah or another ghost, that they were unwelcome there and to go somewhere else. There has been no activity since.

The woman's restroom where Jeremiah likes to taunt women. *Photo Courtesy of Author.*

One gentleman by the name of Ted who was living in the Grand Hotel in the 1980s, before the renovation, told us a story of an experience he had. As he left the room that he used as his bedroom and went out into the hallway to go into the room that he used as his studio to work on one of his pieces, he looked towards the balcony. In the hallway, he saw four men sitting around a table playing poker. He knew he was the only living person in the building, and immediately, knew that those four men were ghosts. He then witnessed one of the men stand up, pull a gun from his holster and shoot another of the men in the head. He then saw the poker game and its players disappear into thin air. Did he witness the death of Jeremiah as a residual haunting in the hotel, right above where the actual killing likely took place?

GHOST TOUR

Most of the Lady Ghost's activity occurs in the Victorian Room. She favors this room probably because of its elegant red velvet curtains, and four-post bed. I have had my own experience in the Victorian Room, while guiding the Old Bisbee Ghost Tour.

It was a Saturday evening during a full moon when we used to take our tours into the Grand Hotel. I was guiding a small group of ten people that evening and took my group up the stairs and into the upstairs hallway. I was describing to my guests how the Lady Ghost is seen walking up the stairs and down the hallway into the Victorian Room. As I was describing where she is seen, I walked into the Victorian Room. Unbeknownst to me, my group had not followed me down the dark hallway and into the haunted room. Instead, they stayed in the hallway at the top of the stairs. I was in the Victorian Room alone and before I could turn around to tell my group they were permitted to enter the room with me, I heard a loud, deep, sigh. I ran out of the room to tell my group what had just happened. Excited and wanting to experience some paranormal activity, they all ran into the room with cameras in hand. Someone turned the lights on and everyone was busy snapping away. Unfortunately, we did not hear the sigh again. As we left the Victorian Room, one gentleman asked if he could stay inside to take photos while no one else was in the room. I granted him permission to do so and I waited for him on the steps. After thirty seconds, he came running out of the Victorian Room as fast as his feet would take him. He imitated the sigh I had heard and asked, "Is that what you heard, when you were in the room by yourself?"

"That is exactly what I heard!" I responded with excitement, happy to know that this gentleman verified to me what I knew I'd heard!

On another tour that I was supervising, we had a group of ten sorority girls join us for a night of ghostly tales. Our newest tour guide was leading the group, and I was on the tour to supervise her first official tour. That evening the Victorian Room was vacant, so we took the girls inside. As our guide was telling the tales of the Lady Ghost in the darkened room, we heard three loud bangs on the window by the bed. The girls ran out of the room screaming, while the guide and I remained. We looked out the window and saw no one there. This was the most profound paranormal experience we had ever had on a tour to date, but the night was still young.

We managed to get the girls back into the Victorian Room and the guide continued telling the spooky tales of the events which occur within its walls. We turned on the lights and stationed two girls by the light switch so that they could turn the lights off after we were finished telling the stories. Before we finished though, the two girls by the light switch started screaming. We calmed them down and asked them what had happened. "We heard someone whisper in our ears, 'this place is scary and you better get out,'" one of the girls said, while trying hard not to cry.

We appeased the ghosts and left the Victorian Room.

My parents came to visit Bisbee and decided to stay at the Bisbee Grand Hotel. They happened to get the Victorian Room. One night they were watching TV and all of a sudden the TV got blurry and then turned to static. Thinking it was nothing, they decided they had had enough TV for the night and decided to go to bed. During the night, my mother woke up to a female voice whispering in her ear, "Heeeeeellllloooooo."

INN AT CASTLE ROCK
Type of Hauntings:
Residual, Intelligent

HISTORY

In 1895, the first mayor of Bisbee built a boarding house at 112 Tombstone Canyon, on the site of what was the first water well in Bisbee. It is also the site of the first mine where silver was found in

Bisbee. It was used as a boarding house during Bisbee's heyday. The single room occupancies were combined to make small apartments in the 1930s because the miners who had families needed more living space. In the 1980s, it was bought and turned into a Bed and Breakfast. The town's original water well is currently in the dining room of the Inn at Castle Rock.

PARANORMAL ACTIVITY

There are three rooms at the Inn at Castle Rock that are the most haunted. Those are the rooms: Crying Shame, Tasmania and Return to Paradise. In the 1930s, these rooms were all one apartment. It is believed that a miner staying in the apartment was cleaning his gun while sitting at the window. The gun went off and accidentally hit and killed a women walking across the street. It is said that her ghost wanders the Inn looking for the man who killed her. In these three rooms, lights go on and off by themselves, people feel their hair being touched, and voices are heard but no one is there.

The original well, located in the dining room, was believed to be the cause of the drowning of a little boy. His ghost is thought to haunt the Inn at Castle Rock. He pulls little pranks like hiding money, and moving around important papers. Though the owner said he is a good boy, since he always returns the money and paperwork a couple days after they disappear.

Before the Boarding House was built, the site was frequented by Native Americans because of its water source. Guests have claimed to see the ghost of a lost Native American roaming the garden in the back of the building.

Employees have claimed that they hear their names being called, and no one is there. Doors of vacant rooms open by themselves, and the lights turn on by themselves.

GHOST TOUR

On one of our tours we saw what looked like a lit candle floating around one of the rooms, as if an invisible person was carrying it and wandering about looking for something that had been lost years ago. As we walked past the building, the candlelight disappeared.

OLIVER HOUSE
Types of Hauntings:
Residual, Intelligent, Portal

HISTORY

At least twenty-six deaths have occurred in what is arguably the most haunted place in Old Bisbee, the Oliver House. Edith Oliver, the wife of Henry Oliver, a big shot mining tycoon, built the Oliver House in 1908. It was used as a boarding house for the mining executives and later for the miners as well. It was built using bricks so that it would not burn down, since fires were not uncommon in Bisbee. In the mid 1980s, Dennis Schranz bought the property. When he bought the house he did not believe in ghosts. After his first night there, he did! Today, it is a Bed and Breakfast, though I like to refer to it as a Dead and Breakfast.

The Oliver House is believed to be one of the most haunted buildings in Arizona. *Photo Courtesy of Author.*

PARANORMAL ACTIVITY

In Room 13, doors open and close by themselves, there are sounds of running water, footsteps, creaking hinges, people talking, and cold spots. It is believed that this was Nat Anderson's room. Nat was a miner, who was having an affair with the wife of the man to whom he owed money. On the night of February 22nd, 1920, Nat was shot at the top of the staircase. It is believed that the man he owed money to, the husband of the lady he was having the affair with, is the one that killed him. The murder was never solved.

We have a town radio station in Bisbee called KPRP. There is a story of one of our local DJs whose friend bet him $100 dollars to spend the night in Nat's room. The DJ took the bet thinking he was going to make a quick hundred bucks. He did not believe in ghosts and was the ultimate skeptic. He checked in, unlocked the door to Room 13, opened it, and saw a full-body apparition standing in front of him. He got so scared that he immediately shut the door, checked out, and gave his friend the money stating that he now believed in ghosts.

A room, once called The Blue Room, was believed to be the scene of another murder due to adultery. In 1932, a local police officer caught his wife having an affair with another man. The police officer killed his wife, her lover, and then went around the rest of the house shooting everyone he could. The gun was then turned on himself.

One of the managers has heard footsteps in the room above his. His children, who were visiting him, heard furniture being moved in the room above theirs. Yet, when they searched the house, no one was there.

One Thursday afternoon, a paranormal investigation group was in the Oliver House doing EVP work. Everyone left and the house was completely empty while they let the recorders run. Upon returning, they listened to the EVPs they recorded. What was recorded was a female voice saying, "I want some BBQ." What the paranormal investigators didn't know was that on Thursday evenings, during the summer, the manager used to have BBQs and invited his friends to the Oliver House. The ghost whose voice was recorded on the EVP knew about the BBQ and was ready to chow down!

GHOST TOUR

In a room upstairs, with a fantastic view of Bisbee, there is believed to be a portal. The portal can be felt in the dead center of the room. On one of our Ghost Tours we took a group inside the Oliver House. We went into the portal room and I along with the majority of the guests felt the portal. We felt a cold spot in the center of the room, and we placed our hands there to absorb its powers. Soon, some of our hands started to tingle, and the tingles moved slowly up our arms. I moved my hand away, and the tingles immediately stopped.

There used to be what was called the Grandma Room. A previous owner named it this because guests claimed to see the apparition of a little old lady sitting in a rocking chair that was placed in the corner of the room. She would make the chair rock back and forth and would apparently make the broken coo-coo clock go off at 2 a.m. on nights that her apparition had been seen.

When the new owners bought the building, they changed the name of the room, threw away the rocking chair and the coo-coo clock, and the Grandma Ghost was very upset. There

A photo taken in Nat Anderson's room of the mirror on the wall. In the reflection is the window on the opposite side of the room. In the reflections, there appears to be the ghost of a woman peering into the window. Nat's room is on the top floor and there is no balcony, so whoever was standing there, they had to be floating! *Photo taken by Liese Krauser.*

Close up of the Oliver House Ghost Photo with an arrow pointing to the image of a woman peering into the window. *Photo taken by Liese Krauser.*

was a family staying at the Oliver House with their three-year-old little boy. His parents tucked him into bed and then went downstairs to socialize with the other guests that were in the house. An hour later, the little boy came running down the stairs crying hysterically. His parents calmed him down and asked him what had happened. He responded, "The little old lady bopped me on the head." Thinking he just had a bad dream, his parents calmed him down, took him back up to bed, and to their astonishment the next day he woke up with a giant black and blue mark on his forehead.

BISBEE INN/ HOTEL LAMORE

The original building burnt down in 1915; this one was built afterwards. One thing the Bisbee Inn/Hotel LaMore does not lack and that is paranormal activity! *Photo Courtesy of Author.*

Types of Hauntings: Residual, Intelligent

HISTORY

In early photographs of Chihuahua Hill, also known as "B" Hill, you can spot two wooden structures where the Bisbee Inn/Hotel LaMore now stands. Directories in 1905 describe these buildings as housing "rooms" and "furnished rooms." These rooms were most likely used by the miners of the day.

The Bisbee Inn, also known as, Hotel LaMore, was built in 1916, on the foundation of those wooden structures that burned down in a fire. At the time of its opening, in 1917, it was considered one of the most modern hotels in Bisbee. The Inn had twenty-four rooms to accommodate guests with rates ranging from $2 a day to $8 a week. Between then and now, it has changed hands many times, as well as functions. In the 1940s, the building was converted to an apartment building with two-room apartments. In the 1960s, it was a training center for the Peace Corps. In 1982, it was restored to its historic status and has been a hotel ever since.

PARANORMAL ACTIVITY

The Bisbee Inn is infamous for its ghostly activity and people from all over the world stay here to experience it. It is believed that one of the ghosts was once a mortal who perished in the original building's fire.

Room 15, which is the middle European room on the second floor, has a ghost that likes to rest in bed next to its guests. It is unknown if this ghost is a male or female, but it gets into bed with both male and female guests. When the guests staying there feel someone climb into bed with them, and they jump out of bed, they claim to see an indentation of a body on the mattress.

Room 11, which is also on the second floor, has had guests' toiletries thrown off the shelf and the bathroom door slam shut. A gentleman, who always stayed in that room while golfing in nearby Naco, had this happen to him on three separate occasions. The last time it happened, he told the owners he could no longer stay at their establishment because the paranormal activity was too much for him to handle.

The first time I came to visit Bisbee, I stayed in this room with my husband and our Shih Tzu, Gizmo. One day, after we returned from shopping, we unlocked the door and opened it as Gizmo leaped off the bed, ran out of the room and dashed down the stairs as fast as he could. My husband had to catch him as he made a mad dash down the stairs. Did Gizmo see the ghost that haunts Room 11? Over a year later, my sister stayed in Room 11 on her first trip to Bisbee to participate in our first Paranormal Weekend. She put her toothpaste on the shelf above the sink, went out for the day, came back and the cap on her toothpaste had come off the tube and was sitting neatly next to it on the shelf.

The ghost of a miner has been seen on this staircase.
Photo Courtesy of Author.

Bisbee is a town of animal lovers, and because of that, we have a vast population of homeless animals, mostly feral cats. The building next door to the Bisbee Inn used to be the LaMore Saloon. There was a feral cat that used to try to sneak into the hotel in the wintertime to warm up. The owner did not want the cat in the hotel, but did not mind if it hung out in the saloon. So, she would shoo it out of the hotel and the cat would find its way into the Saloon. One day it was shooed out of the hotel, went next door to the saloon, went downstairs, and then found its way into the liquor storage room. The poor cat got locked in the storage room and starved to death. It was a few days after they found the dead cat's body that Room 23, at the Bisbee Inn, started getting reports of a ghost cat. Room 23 is really Room 13, and patrons feel the cat walk on the bed and curl up next to them while they are sleeping. Some said that they could feel it purring in the middle of the night. Children staying in the room claim to have seen the ghost cat and say it is a calico cat. After discussions with the owner, we discovered that indeed the cat was a calico cat.

My favorite ghost in Bisbee haunts Room 23 at the Bisbee Inn/Hotel LaMore; it is that of the ghost cat. *Photo Courtesy of Author.*

I had two friends who stayed in Room 23, at the Bisbee Inn. One said that she heard a cat walk from the door to the bathroom. Curious to see the cat, she got out of bed, turned on the light in the bathroom and saw nothing there. The other friend woke up to a cat scratching at the window. She felt at the time that it might also be a tree scratching against the window, only to discover the next morning, that there are no trees surrounding the building.

There is also believed to be the ghost of a man that has been seen on the back staircase, off the second floor by the European rooms. He is believed to be a miner. When he has been spotted, everyone describes him as wearing a vest, jeans that he tucks into his boots, and having dirty long hair. Guests who have seen him state that he is extremely handsome. The reason he is seen only on that staircase is unknown.

The most active ghost at the Bisbee Inn is the Lady in White. She is your stereotypical ghost. She wears a long white gown and has flowing long white hair. She roams the hotel and when she is near, patrons have smelled lilacs. The Lady in White saved the lives of three boys during the monsoon season in the 1950s. The three boys got out of a movie show at the Lyric Theater and were running home because it was raining when the show let out. They ran up OK Street, up the steps next to the Bisbee Inn and turned left, down the back alleyway. When they turned the corner, the Lady in White walked through the back door and outstretched her arm. She put her hand out in the STOP position. The boys got so frightened they turned around and started to run back down the steps. At that moment a rockslide occurred from the hill above. The boys believe that the Lady in White saved their lives that day. Repairs made to the wall after the rockslide can still be seen to this day.

Some people also report that she seems to favor Rooms 7 and 12 in the building. There have been reports of guests seeing her hover in the corner of their room looking very beautiful and angelic. Other strange anomalies have taken place at the Bisbee Inn/Hotel LaMore. Some of these include glowing balls of light being seen on the first floor near the desk area, guests have heard knocks on walls, footsteps on the stairs, the rocking chair upstairs sometimes will start rocking by itself, and the scent of carbolic acid has been sensed as well.

In June of 2008, the Old Bisbee Ghost Tour placed a "Ghost Boooooook" in the lobby of the Bisbee Inn. Some paranormal experiences which guests have written in the book include:

Room 5—one guest felt a cold tingle enter their back and leave through their front

Room 7—the bathroom door opened by itself; footsteps going up and down the staircase yet no one was there

Room 9— doorknob was seen and heard jiggling

Room 10—a coffee cup shattered and the guests claimed it was the fault of the ghost; heard noises like cats scratching at the door

Room 11—an unexplained gold light was seen; felt something pull the covers off their feet in the middle of the night

Room 23—cat toys moved; cat jumping from the headboard onto the bed; heard the rocking chair in the hallway start to creak in the middle of the night

Upstairs Hallway— the smell of lavender hovering around the rocking chair in the upstairs hallway

Stairs—footsteps on the stairs and when guest went to take photographs and their camera battery died as they descended upon the staircase

Other Happenings—a gust of wind when all the windows and doors were closed; clothes moved in the middle of the night; cold spots and warm spots felt; a room key was moved from the desk to the top of the door frame

GHOST TOUR

During one of our ghost tours, we were allowed to go inside the Bisbee Inn. Two girls on the tour were staying in Room 7. They were going to use the restroom in their room while the other guests were taking the tour and looking around the haunted hotel.

Before leaving for the Ghost Tour, the girls left the lights in their room on. When they went back to use the restroom, the lights in their room were off. Too scared to use the restroom in their room after discovering the lights were turned off, they came running down the stairs to tell the rest of the guests on the tour what had happened. They were terrified to stay the night, but I assured them that most of the ghosts in Bisbee were friendly and to not worry too much.

On another ghost tour when we were able to go inside, a group of guests went to the second floor of the hotel and noticed that the rocking chair was rocking by itself. Thinking that one of the other guests knocked into it, they thought nothing of the incident, but upon returning to the rocking chair a few moments later, it was still rocking, as if an unseen person was sitting in it.

On a tour in the summer of 2009, the Bisbee Inn only had two rooms occupied. The guests in the rooms were taking the Old Bisbee Ghost Tour and let us in to explore the haunted building. When it was time to go, the Ghost Host did a head count and came up two short, so one of the guests who was staying at the hotel said that she would go in to see if she could round up the missing guests. While in the kitchen and dining area she heard people talking upstairs. Thinking that the voices belonged to the missing guests, she went upstairs and no one was there. She knocked on the door of her brother-in-law's room, who had decided not to take the tour, and was the only other person (besides our two missing guests) in the hotel. He claimed that he did not hear anyone talking or voices. The guest came outside to discover that the Ghost Host miscounted and everyone on the tour was there. She was dumbfounded by this and couldn't figure out where the voices she had heard came from.

GHOST HUNT

Our first ever Paranormal and Ghost Hunting Weekend took place at the Bisbee Inn/Hotel LaMore. A couple of weeks prior to the arrival of our guests, the members of the International Community of Paranormal Investigation and Research came to the Bisbee Inn/Hotel LaMore for a preliminary investigation. The only other people in the building besides the investigators were a mother and her little girl, both of whom were very excited to be staying at a haunted hotel during an investigation. IR cameras were set up in the hallway facing the stairs where the miner ghost is seen. EVP recorders were set up around the building. In Room 23, we hung a glow stick from a piece of string and then dangled it from the bathroom doorknob. It, too, had an IR camera recording it. Some of us had our EMF detectors ready, others had dowsing rods, and everyone was energized for a night of paranormal activity.

We were teamed up and each team went throughout the building trying to catch evidence. In Room 7, I was sitting on the bed with another investigator; my head was on the bed's headboard and, all of a sudden, it started to vibrate. We immediately asked for a presence to make itself known to us, and suddenly, there was a knock on the wall. We believe that this was most likely the Lady in White since she is the ghost that favors Room 7.

Later that evening, the three of us moved down the hallway to Room 23, which is the room where the ghost cat has been felt, heard, and seen. It was in this room where we had hung the glow stick from the doorknob. After we entered the room, we shut the door and one of the investigators and I sat on the bed. Christy, the leader of the group was changing the disk in the video recorder; as she did this, she readjusted the angle of the camera. While looking through the viewfinder, she saw that the glow stick was swinging from side to side, as if a cat was swatting and playing with it, like it would a cat toy.

CITY PARK

City Park as it looks today. *Photo Courtesy of Author.*

The old cemetery as it looked in the 1880s. *Photo courtesy of the Bisbee Mining and Historical Museum.*

Type of Hauntings: Residual, Intellectual

HISTORY

City Park is located on Brewery Gulch. It is a fun spot to play basketball, or enjoy some music or a theatrical performance taking place on the stage. What is surprising to know is that this sanctuary of youth used to be the Bisbee Cemetery. In the early 1900s, the city felt that the bodies buried there were too close to the water system. There was concern that diseases, like typhoid, would get into the drinking water. So they moved all the marked graves over to the then newly established Evergreen Cemetery that is located on the other side of town.

George Warren who is on the Arizona State Seal and founding father of Bisbee was buried in the corner of the old Bisbee Cemetery. His grave almost went unnoticed until a worker found a little cross in the ground with the name WARREN carved into it. George Warren's body was moved to the Evergreen Cemetery and given a much more elaborate grave than his first one.

Bisbee folklore states that there are estimates that between half a dozen to a dozen bodies are still buried under the concrete

This photograph was taken in July of 2009 during the Old Bisbee Ghost Tour in Bisbee's City Park which used to be the city's cemetery. Many believe the ghosts of children haunt the park to this day. Perhaps this photograph is proof of that. Please note the shadow of a ghost child to the left of the photograph. *Photo courtesy of Jason Caloun.*

park. Due to poor records, if a grave was not marked, the city did not know where to dig.

PARANORMAL ACTIVITY

One of our locals has a daughter who, at the time of the following experience, was 2 1/2 years old. They were playing on the playground equipment in City Park when the daughter went down the slide and focused her attention on the stairs. She said, "Daddy, Daddy, look at the children playing on the stairs." When her father looked over, he saw no children. She, however, ran to the stairs, despite her father's confusion, and started playing on the stairs as if she was playing with other children.

Her father took his time walking over to the stairs, observing his daughter play with these ghost children. When he reached the stairs, she was very upset and came walking down to her father pouting. He asked his daughter what was wrong and she responded, "You scared them all away. They all walked through the wall and are now hiding from you."

The father took his daughter back to the play equipment and they continued playing. A few minutes later, she again went down the slide and called to her father's attention the children playing on the stairs. She ran to the stairs to play with the ghost children. This time her father got so unnerved that he took his daughter and his dog and went to have a drink at St. Elmo's Bar to calm down.

GHOST TOUR

It is not uncommon on our Old Bisbee Ghost Tour to have people feel as if they are getting poked by children while sitting on the stairs. This has happened on numerous occasions. Usually, when guests have this happen to them, they state that it was not a threatening poke, nor did it hurt. It feels more like a child trying to get their attention, and they do so by poking guests in the back.

GHOST HUNT

During a recording for Donovan from K101 in Sierra Vista's Ghost Patrol, we did some EVP recordings in City Park. We were there at 11 p.m. at night, and besides Donovan and myself, there were twelve cheerleaders from the local high school and their chaperone. The girls played the game *Ring A Round the Rosy* to try to entice the ghost children to come out. We did not see any visual ghosts that night, though some of us felt that creepy uneasy feeling during our EVP session at City Park.

After listening to the recording a couple days later, Donovan stated that he caught a man's voice during the EVP session, not children's. Unfortunately, because we were outside, and not in a controlled environment, it was very difficult for us to hear what the man's voice was saying.

ST. ELMO BAR
Type of Hauntings: Residual

HISTORY

St. Elmo Bar was built in 1902 and is the longest continuously running bar in Arizona. They even served through prohibition. There is a mineshaft under the bar that is still accessible today. It is believed that during prohibition, they would sneak booze into the then soda fountain shop through this mineshaft, which runs under the building, and out to the street.

On top of the building, you will see a strange sight. An entire story of another house called the Blair House, which used to stand on Zatatacas Canyon, was brought to St. Elmo. In Bisbee's early years, the bars would often have brothels upstairs. The story goes that the men here were not satisfied with the number of working women upstairs, and decided they needed more room to house more women. In the middle of the night, a group of men went to the Blair House and brought back part of it and placed it on top of the pre existing building on Brewery Gulch.

PARANORMAL ACTIVITY

The current owner bought the bar in 1992. He used to live upstairs on the second floor. During this time, he claims to have heard a man and woman laughing when the bar was closed and he was alone in the building. He wanted proof that his building was haunted. He decided to put powdered lime on the stairs one night in hopes of finding footprints in the morning. His idea was unsuccessful. The paranormal activity grew and grew. He would

St. Elmo's bar is the oldest continuously running bar in the state of Arizona. Some say it served through prohibition. *Photo Courtesy of Author.*

hear the jukebox in the bar go on by itself and play music when the bar was completely closed. He was so frightened by this that he went downstairs and unplugged the jukebox from the wall. When he went back upstairs, he awoke in the wee hours of the morning to hear the unplugged jukebox playing dancing music. When he went downstairs to check on the jukebox, he heard the laughter of his two ghosts. He believes that the ghosts enjoy the modern music the jukebox provides them, and as long as they dance at night while no one is there, he is okay to let them be.

If anyone does see them here at the bar during the day, and dies of fright, he does have lime to cover the body and a mineshaft in which to hide it!

One former bartender at St. Elmo told us a story about his last night working there. He was cleaning up the bar after everyone had left and he heard a beer mug knock against a table, something common among customers when they want a refill of their drink. When the bartender went to where the knocking sound was coming from, it moved to the other side of the bar. He followed it again and the noise moved again. This happened for about fifteen minutes. The Bartender said that he felt that the ghosts did not want him to leave on his last day of employment there.

OK STREET BOARDING HOUSE
Types of Hauntings: Residual

HISTORY

Not far from the Bisbee Inn, on OK Street, stands a building that used to be a boarding house for the miners of Bisbee. It is a three-story poured-concrete building built in the early 1900s. The top floor was where the miner's rooms were; the second floor was the social floor consisting of the kitchen, dining area, baths, and sitting rooms. The first floor, that is partially underground, is where the owners or caretakers of the boarding house are believed to have lived. After the mines closed, the local baker used the bottom floor to bake his goods and the top floors were his family's living quarters. The new owner converted each of the floors into a separate apartment, and now rents to locals.

PARANORMAL ACTIVITY

There was a young couple that moved into the second floor apartment. Shortly after moving in, the wife woke up to footsteps walking around the bed, back and forth, from one side of the bed to the other. A few weeks after that occurrence, the wife woke up to a little girl crying at the end of the bed. She didn't see anyone there, just heard her weeps. This time the wife woke up her husband so he could experience the paranormal activity for himself, but to no avail. He did not hear a thing and told his wife to go back to sleep. She couldn't, the crying was too loud. So she sat up in bed and asked the unseen girl to stop crying because she needed to get up early for work the next morning. As soon as she asked the girl to stop crying, the crying ceased. They also experienced their electrical appliances, such as their stereo, and TV turning on and off by themselves.

The wife decided to talk to the landlord about these paranormal experiences. When she did, the landlord told her that it was a regular occurrence in the building for people to experience paranormal activity such as the wife had experienced. The landlord

This apartment building was once a boarding house for the miners. It appears that one might not have left! *Photo Courtesy of Author.*

stated though that most of the activity occurs on the third floor and not the second floor.

The wife decided to investigate the building further and started interviewing the other occupants. She found out that one occupant was told from a life-long resident of Bisbee, that a gentleman committed suicide in the building after the mines closed. He was distraught over where he would go to find work. This story though has never been verified and no documentation was ever found regarding it.

The couple was planning a much-deserved vacation and asked their friend who lived in the first floor apartment if she could watch their place while they were gone. One evening, their friend was in her living room and heard footsteps walking in the apartment upstairs. Thinking that the apartment was being burglarized, she and her boyfriend hurried upstairs to find the place completely empty. A few days after the first incident, she was in her bedroom and heard footsteps again coming from the second floor apartment. She went inside and again it was empty.

The couple, after hearing these stories upon their return from vacation, decided to move out of the haunted location. They moved into a non-haunted home in the Warren area of Bisbee. Their friend, who remained in the apartment below, said that after they left, she would still hear the ghost walking upstairs.

A new resident moved into the second floor apartment and was asked if anything paranormal had happened to her. She stated that the lamp in the kitchen would be off, and then turn on by itself, or be on and then turn off by itself. She figured the place must be haunted and told the spirit to stop playing with her lamp. Since then, the activity surrounding the lamp has ceased.

BISBEE COURTHOUSE
Type of Haunting:
Residual, Intelligent

HISTORY

In 1931, after the county seat was moved from Tombstone to Bisbee, the county built the Bisbee Courthouse. The courthouse is a perfect example of Art Deco Architecture. The first judge of the courthouse was John Wilson Ross, who served from 1931 until 1943. In the upper floor of the courthouse is where the jail use to be, and is currently used as storage space.

PARANOMAL ACTIVITY

It is the ghost of Judge Ross that is believed to haunt the building. Most of the paranormal phenomena occurs either on the top floor of the building, which used to be the jail and is now used for storage, or in the division 2 courtroom.

One evening, one of the women from the cleaning staff had her daughter with her while she was working. She asked her daughter to go into the division 2 courtroom and to put all the chairs in the up position so it would be easier for her to clean under them. When the cleaning woman went to check in on her daughter, all the chairs were in the down position. The mother asked her daughter who had put the chairs that way and the little girl pointed to the photo of Judge Ross that was on the wall.

The Bisbee Courthouse is a very fine example of Art Deco architecture.
Photo Courtesy of Author.

One of the court's file clerks was on the top floor getting a file from the storage area that used to be the jail. She walked into the room and saw seated in a chair in front of her an elderly gentleman who was all dressed in black. She was so frightened by this encounter, she ran down two flights of stairs and locked the door behind her with a chain. Not realizing, that if indeed she had just seen a ghost, a locked door and chain would do little, since ghosts can and do walk through walls.

Other paranormal activity includes lights flickering on and off by themselves, as well as the elevator running by itself. Employees who work there have also heard footsteps in the halls late at night. Most of the paranormal activity is believed to be caused by the ghost of Judge Ross. When there is a sighting, the ghost is usually wearing a black robe and fits Judge Ross's description. Another theory is that the activity is caused by the ghosts of those who were locked up tight in the old jail on the top floor.

BREWERY GULCH BROTHEL

An old brothel that is being refurbished by the new owners—which may explain the activity has been heightened. *Photo Courtesy of Author.*

Type of Haunting: Residual

HISTORY

Brewery Gulch was infamous in its day for being full of drunks and prostitutes. No dignified man or woman would be seen anywhere on The Gulch. The working-women's cribs would be scattered up and down the street. The workingwomen standing outside their cribs would entice men to pay them a visit. Today most of those old brothels have either fallen to rubble, or have been turned into cute little homes. If one takes a ride up Brewery Gulch and looks carefully, you can see sets of stairs every five or six feet on people's property. These stairs are the remains of the old brothels. The stairs lead the men to the women's rooms.

PARANORMAL ACTIVITY

There was apparently one brothel in town that catered to only African-American men. The women who worked there were Swedish immigrants brought to America for the sole purpose of making money as prostitutes. These women were told that their only customers in this particular brothel in Bisbee were to be African-American men. This made all the other men in Bisbee angry and determined. One night, they went to the brothel and murdered almost all the prostitutes who were working there. If they couldn't enjoy their services, too, than no one could!

The abandoned brick building that used to be the brothel still stands two stories tall. Late at night, men who have walked past the building, have seen the shadows of women standing in mid air, on what would have been their balconies. These men claim that they can also hear the women whistling to them from above. These ghostly women of the evening are still trying to entice men to come in for some pleasure a hundred years after they have been murdered!

AUDREY'S INN
Type of Haunting: Residual

HISTORY

Audrey's Inn is an adorably cute little bed and breakfast located right in the center of town. The building was built in 1904. It is three stories tall because the original builder wanted it to withstand the annual flooding of Brewery Avenue. The first floor used to be a saloon, the second floor was used as rental offices, and the third floor housed a "Businessman's Club" used for lodging. The first floor saloon was called "The Shattuck" and was named after the owner of the building. At the time it was a very elite saloon. It had crystal chandeliers, a mahogany bar with brass foot rails, mirrors that covered all the walls and gambling tables. Bartenders were dressed to the nines, as were the dealers. Women were not allowed and rowdiness was not tolerated. In 1907, a Liquor Control act was passed, and Shattuck closed down the games and the club on the third floor. The third floor was then used as a lodging house. In 1914, when Prohibition became the law, Shattuck closed down his saloon for good.

PARANORMAL ACTIVITY

Before buying the building, the owner used to stay here as a guest. In what is now the Cowboy Suite, she and her husband heard the sounds of children running up and down the hallways above them in what is now the Chinese Suite. After buying the building, they opened it up as a hotel and condos. Sometimes they get complaints from guests, who stay in the Cowboy Suite, about the children running upstairs, usually when no children are staying at the hotel. Audrey states that the best time to hear the children are between 2 a.m. and 4 a.m. on nights of the full moon.

The bottom floor used to be the bar and recently houses Mexico Lindo's Takeout. The owner and one of their workers were looking out the window one afternoon and saw a man walk up to the door. He peered inside, and then took a few steps back. As he stepped back, he disappeared. They both ran to the window and to their shock he was not anywhere to be seen. They believe that he is waiting for his favorite bar to reopen its doors again.

BISBEE REPERTORY THEATER
Type of Haunting: Residual

HISTORY

The Bisbee Repertory Theater was originally built in the early 1900s and its original use was as a church. It sat vacant for many years before it was completely renovated and transformed into the dinner theater it is today. It is a popular place to have a meal and see the latest musical show performed by local Bisbeeites. Though, don't be surprised if you see more than what you bargained for! This theater is haunted!

There is a theater superstition that states that you must leave a light on in the center of the stage of a darkened empty theater. It is referred to as a Ghost Light. If you fail to leave a Ghost Light on, it is believed that a ghost will take residence in the theater. If they can't see due to the darkness left by having no light, they cause mischief and pranks on the thespians and stagehands. Maybe the Repertory Theater forgot to leave on their Ghost Light!

PARANORMAL ACTIVITY

You shouldn't be fooled by its pretty architecture. Behind those walls actors have seen ghosts. The spirit will walk back and forth across the stage, through the seats of the aisles and disappear into thin air. Actors also get a creepy feeling, as if they are being watched when they are in the dressing room, getting ready for their performance.

Could this ghost be a priest, or clergyman who used to work at the building when it was a church? Or could it be a local ghost from a neighboring building who enjoys going to the theater to see a show? Or maybe it is a performer who never got to fulfill his destiny of being on the big stage. Perhaps now he feels it's his chance to shine?

BISBEE CONVENTION CENTER
Type of Haunting: Residual

HISTORY

The original building that stood here burned down in 1938. The following year, the Phelps Dodge Mercantile was built on the site, designed and overseen by world-renowned art deco designer Del Webb. It was Webb's first commercial building. When it was the Phelps Dodge Mercantile, the building was filled with everything the miners and their families could want or need, from mining supplies to sewing supplies, to clothing. Located on the top floor, are now offices and on the first floor, you will find treats for your eyes and taste buds. Though when the doors are locked late at night, and there is no one there but the cleaning crew, strange paranormal activity occurs.

PARANORMAL ACTIVITY

One employee of the restaurant was working late cleaning up and she had to go into the basement to retrieve some boxes. She was by herself, but felt as if she was not alone. She walked down the stairs and felt a chill go down her spine. She then felt a man breathe on her neck. She not only felt his warm breath, but she heard it, too.

Another employee was mopping the floors after the building had been closed for the night. She was on the first floor working when she heard a radio playing music. When she went in the direction of the music, and thought she was getting close to it, it moved to the other side of the building. When she followed it to the other side of the building, it moved again to another location. This same occurrence happened to another employee working late at night by himself in the building. He heard a high-pitched beeping sound. He went to find it, and as he got near to where the sound was coming from, it moved. He followed it again, and when he got close it moved again.

In the coffee shop, a long-time employee has seen the ghost of a little girl with blond hair and a blue dress dart around the corners and doorways. He has seen her on multiple occasions out of the corner of his eye, though he does not know who she is or what she is doing. He said that she is not frightening or scary, and just seems to want to play a little game of hide and seek.

Employees of the building have also claimed to hear whispers of people coming from all floors of the building when no one is there, as well as footsteps.

A woman who use to work in the building years ago, before its current owner purchased it, told us that one day she was walking up the creepy back staircase from the first floor to the upper floor. At the top of the stairs she saw the ghost of an elderly woman sitting in a chair. As she went further up the staircase, the lady disappeared. She saw this woman a few times before mentioning it to one of her fellow employees. They asked her what had taken so long for her to mention the ghost at the top of the staircase.

Could the miners of long ago still be haunting the building? Or could it be the ghost of someone who perished in the fire of the original structure?

MITCHEL FAMILY MORTUARY

What are now art galleries, used to be the Mitchel Family Mortuary. *Photo Courtesy of Author.*

Type of Haunting: Intelligent

HISTORY

You would not know by looking at the building located at 76 Main Street that it was once a Mortuary. The white brick building used to be the place where Bisbeeites came to pay their last respects to friends, family, and colleagues before burying them, most presumably, at the Evergreen Cemetery. The mortuary was divided up into three separate stores after the mortuary closed down. Walls were put in to partition the stores from one another. The original entrance is where the middle shop is today.

PARANORMAL ACTIVITY

One of the previous renters of the middle storefront used to rent the old Miners and Merchants Bank and left it due to paranormal activity to move farther down to 76 Main Street. He claimed that while he was in the basement of the old bank, where the vaults and his office were located, he would hear the noises of objects breaking and bodies being dragged around from the main floor. Of course, when he went upstairs nothing was broken and no one was there. Since he heard these residual noises every night, he got spooked and wanted to move his shop. He downsized and moved into the former mortuary.

After he moved into his new smaller shop, he turned the room in the back into his office. After closing for the day, he would go into his office to start doing his paperwork. While counting his money, he started to hear little footsteps coming from the stairs leading up to his shop's front door. This always happened late at night after he was closed for the day. He went to the door, thinking a child was playing on the other side, and of course, no one was there. This would happen night after night, after night. He cut his losses and decided to move to Las Vegas.

Soon after, an artist used the space as an art gallery. The artist's assistant was working late one night. She heard footsteps and could not tell where they were coming from. Searching the entire building, she could not find a source for those mysterious footsteps. That artist quickly moved out due to the paranormal occurrences, too.

The storefront was vacant for a few months and when I would bring the Old Bisbee Ghost Tour by, I would tell my guests that the space was available for rent, ghosts included. Two women on the tour thought this was a great idea, went home from their trip to Bisbee and told their mom about the haunted location. The woman immediately sold her house, moved to Bisbee, and rented the space.

One night, she was working really late in the gallery, getting it ready for her grand opening. At around 11 p.m., she decided to call it a day. As she was driving home, she drove past her gallery. She looked at it to admire her work and saw the ghost of a little girl sitting on the front steps. The little girl was wearing a dress with a white pinafore. As the renter blinked to make sure she was not seeing things, she noticed that the little girl slowly vanished right before her eyes.

The next time her daughters came to town, they decided to put a digital recorder in their mother's new gallery to try to catch some EVPs. The daughters, being amateur ghost hunters, felt that this was a great opportunity to collect some evidence. They left the recorder running overnight, and when they listened to it the next day they were shocked. At 3 a.m., the recorder picked up the sound of a ball bouncing against the wall, over and over again. It would then sound like the ball started bouncing away from the wall, followed by the sound of little footsteps trying to retrieve it. After that, the sound of the ball bouncing against the wall could be heard again.

October approached and it was Halloween. The renter's daughters were guests for our Haunted Halloween Weekend, which included a séance in the tower of the Copper Queen Hotel. Their mother decided to join her daughters in the séance having never done anything like that before, and thinking it might be a good way to make contact with the ghost that haunted her gallery.

The medium at the séance placed objects on a table in the corner of the room. These objects were there for the spirits to play with, so they could show the participants that they were present in the room. The participants kept asking the spirits for a sign and nothing was happening. A husband, who had been dragged to the séance under protest, verbally stated, "If anyone is in this room, please ring a bell or something." Immediately, one of the bells placed on the table in the corner of the room rang.

The mediums used a pendulum to ask yes and no questions. They asked if the spirit was one who haunts the Copper Queen Hotel, and the pendulum said, "no." They asked if it was a spirit from another one of the hotels in town and the pendulum said, "no," again. The mother chimed in and asked if the spirit was that of the little girl who haunts her gallery and the pendulum swayed, "yes."

During the séance, one of the mediums was using a technique called automatic writing, which invites a spirit to write messages on paper using the medium's hand. She would write something and then hand the piece of paper to the other medium with the pendulum and she would interpret what was written. Though, this time when the medium started to do the automatic writing, she handed the piece of paper to the mother.

On the paper it said, "My blue ball makes me happy."

What we eventually learned is that the Mitchell family, whose funeral home was on the site of the new gallery, had a seven-year-old daughter who died in a fire. The woman believes that it is her ghost that haunts her art gallery. And if she comes into the gallery late at night and plays with her blue ball, that is OK with her!

SILVER KING HOTEL
Type of Haunting: Intelligent

HISTORY

The Silver King Hotel was built on top of a mine and was used as a boarding house for the miners. After the mines closed, it was turned into a hotel. There is a lot of violence that is associated with the Silver King. A terrible incident in the 1970s occurred here when two teenagers were throwing water balloons out of a second-story window. One of the water balloons hit a biker's motorcycle, which made the biker very upset. He came up the stairs and stabbed one of the boys to death.

Today, it is used as a hotel or as short-term apartments—though, many who have had apartments here, claim that they leave because of the paranormal activity.

PARANORMAL ACTIVITY

Residents and guests alike will hear noises in the dead of morning. Mostly they hear what sounds like people going up and down the stairs. This might be a normal occurrence in a hotel but when people described it to us, they said it sounded like twenty or more people running up and down the stairs. That would not be normal for this building since they do not have accommodations for that many people.

One local resident lived in the Silver King when she first moved to Bisbee. She lived in Room 3. Room 3 was three boarding rooms until they tore down the dividing walls to make it into one apartment. One night, she had gone to the grocery store and had left a paper bag of food on her table. In the middle of the night, she awoke to the noises of someone rustling through her bag of groceries. She got up, thinking someone might have broken into her apartment, or that some animal was trying to steal her food. As she neared the kitchen table that had the grocery bag on it, she noticed that nothing was there and the noises had stopped.

During her stay at the Silver King, her dog would watch an unseen being in the corner of the room. The dog's head would move and his eyes would not leave the ghost. There have also been occurrences involving men doing work in the building. Their tools would go missing, and would always turn up in the boiler room. The reason is unknown.

OPERA DRIVE BROTHEL
Type of Haunting: Intelligent

HISTORY

The history of this building is a bit vague. Built in the early 1900s, at 140B Opera Drive, this building was believed to have been a brothel during Bisbee's mining days. The top floor was where the Madam was believed to have lived, and the bottom floors were where the girls were believed to work their trade.

It has since been converted into an apartment building. The top floor, where the Madam lived is now two separate apartments, and the bottom floors are used for storage.

PARANORMAL ACTIVITY

It appears that the Madam of the brothel still haunts her house of ill repute, and she hates it when the residents who live there keep their apartments in an untidy condition. One night, a past resident had left her sink full of dirty dishes. They were piled high on top of one another. She awoke in the middle of the night to the sink faucet going at full blast. She found her way into the kitchen, turned it off and went back to sleep. A half hour later she heard it turn on again. When she walked into the kitchen, both the hot and cold water were turned on all the way. She made a promise out loud to the Madam that she would clean the dishes in the morning. The faucets remained off for the duration of the night. Of course, in the morning, she cleaned the dishes to please the unseen Madam. After that, she always tried to clean the dirty dishes as to not annoy the Madam's ghost.

This same resident would see the ghost on occasion, usually out of the corner of her eye. She said that she wore a blue dress and had gray hair. She has since moved out, and the new resident of the apartment told us that he, too, has seen the ghost of the Madam. He said that he often sees her out of the corner of his eye and knows to keep the apartment *spic and span*, cleaning his dishes after he uses them so as not to anger the ghost of the Madam.

HOTEL SAN RAMON
Type of Hauntings: Residual, Intelligent

HISTORY

This lovely Bed and Breakfast, built in 1902, has bright airy rooms that are beautifully decorated with the finest furnishings. Since its opening, it has been a grocery store, Western Union office, barbershop, pharmacy, ice cream parlor, miners bath house, Moose Lodge, offices for the Bisbee Fuel and Feed, and the home of the El Minuto Tortilla Factory.

The current owner's great-grandfather was the proprietor of the Central Pharmacy, which was located in this same building

The ghost of a tall gentlemen is said to awaken female guests while they sleep. *Photo Courtesy of Author.*

during the early 1900s. His great-grandson bought the building in 2006 and opened the Hotel San Ramon, and under it, Santiago's Mexican Restaurant.

PARANORMAL ACTIVITY

Tamara, who is one of the owners and the manager of the establishment, has had paranormal experiences during the short time she has owned it. After the beds were made in Room 1, Tamara would turn around, or leave the room. Upon her return, there would be an imprint on the bed as if someone had been sitting on it. She would straighten out the comforter, check up on the other rooms, come back to that room, and the imprint would be there again. Sometimes, when walking up the staircase to get to the hotel from the ground level, she would hear a set of footsteps following her up.

Also in Room 1, a patron was awakened in the middle of the night to an apparition of a ghost trying on her husband's clothes. Her husband is a tall gentleman, which is why they reserved Room 1. It has a king-size bed and could accommodate his tall stature. Her recollection of the ghost was that he was just as tall as her husband. He must have had a hard time finding clothes that fit him, because she asked the spirit, "What are you doing?" and it responded, "I am tall; your husband is tall, and it is hard to find clothing for us."

Another patron staying with her family in Room 6 saw a tall apparition walk through the door into the bathroom and then disappear.

We had a guest on the Old Bisbee Ghost Tour that was staying in Room 6. After the tour, she went back to her room to go to sleep. During the night, she felt that the pillows were too big and wanted to see if there were any smaller ones. She opened her eyes, looked up, and there was a guy standing by the TV. He had on a backpack of some sort, a long jacket, and a hat. She described him as being really tall. She could not see his face, only the coat and hat. The guest was shocked and screamed and started crying. She immediately drew a picture of what she had seen so that she wouldn't forget it.

A family, consisting of a husband, wife, and their two daughters, had taken the Old Bisbee Ghost Tour. They, too, were staying in Room 6, at the Hotel San Ramon. After the tour, they went back to the hotel to go to sleep. The wife tucked the girls into bed as her husband took a shower in the bathroom. After his shower, the husband got into bed and started dozing off while his wife cleaned up after him by taking his used towels, folding them neatly, and putting them over the shower rod to dry overnight. After brushing her teeth she went to bed. At 3 a.m., the wife had to use the restroom. She got up, turned on the lights in the bathroom, and the towels, which she had neatly folded and put on the shower rod to dry, were now in the tub, in the sink, and in the toilet

The wife, thinking that her husband was playing a practical joke on her, woke him up, and asked if he had done that to the towels. He took a look and responded that he had not. Their girls were still tucked in and they knew that they had not awoken during the night. Being frightened and not knowing what to do, the husband and wife sat up in bed and were discussing whether or not they should pack their bags and drive back home to Phoenix, at three o'clock in the morning. Suddenly they heard a male voice whisper in their ears, "I am sorry."

SHADY DELL

A view of from the Evergreen Cemetery looking at the backside of the Shady Dell. The most haunted trailers are the ones that are adjacent to the cemetery. *Photo Courtesy of Author.*

Type of Hauntings: Residual, Intelligent

HISTORY

If you want the most unique lodging experience in Arizona, you must spend a night or two at the Shady Dell. As you walk on the property, you are immediately taken back to the 1950s. All the accommodations at the Shady Dell are fully restored vintage aluminum travel trailers. Each trailer is furnished with original and replicated antiques, have the original working kitchen appliances, and have a little astro-turf front yard—some adorned with pink flamingos. There is also a vintage boat and bus with a Tiki theme to accommodate weary travelers.

The Shady Dell was started by a collector of vintage trailers. He opened the Shady Dell to share his love for unique collectables. In 2008, Justin and Jennifer bought the park and took over Dot's Diner, which is a 1950 vintage trailer turned into a quaint and cozy restaurant. Dot's Diner was brought on the back of a flatbed truck from the corner of Topanga Canyon and Ventura Boulevard in Los Angeles to the Shady Dell in Bisbee.

PARANORMAL ACTIVITY

The location of the Shady Dell might explain some of its paranormal activity. The little trailer park nestles right up against Bisbee's Evergreen Cemetery. The trailers that get all of the paranormal activity are those closest to the cemetery.

Trailer 5, the 1951 Mansion, is a 33-foot-long trailer with a cute little side yard. While in the yard, you have a great view of the cemetery and lots of children's graves. So it should be no shocker when guests staying there hear a little girl crying in the yard. Others have heard, what they describe, as the sounds of children playing coming from the side yard.

A couple staying in Trailer 9, a 1957 Airfloat Trailer, awoke to the vintage TV turning on by itself. They could smell cigarette smoke. They sat up in bed, looked in the direction of the TV, and saw the shape of two figures sitting on the sofa. They described them as wearing old-style clothing and each was wearing a hat. The gentleman staying in the trailer got out of bed and turned off the TV. The figures disappeared, but the smell from their cigarettes lingered.

The most unique trailer on the property isn't a trailer at all. It is a 1947 Chris Craft Yacht, and many have seen the ghost of a gentleman sitting on its deck. The ghost is described as being an elderly man with a white beard. Numerous guests have seen him quite frequently. One evening the owner of the Shady Dell was straightening up and locking up the Yacht for the night. She placed a small ceramic dish shaped like a teapot straight in front of the percolator. She headed back to the office and noticed that she left the lights on. She went back to the boat and turned them off. As she did, she noticed that the dish had been turned 45 degrees. It spooked her so badly that to this day she won't go into the Yacht after dark.

The trailer that has the most recent activity would be that of Trailer 4, the 1950 Spartanette. Guests claim to hear the sounds of someone walking through the trailer late at night. A mother and daughter have stayed there twice, and both times experienced the same activity. They bought some groceries, and put them in the refrigerator. The setting on the refrigerator was set to number 3, as it always is. In the morning, their food had been frozen as the temperature setting mysteriously moved from number 3 to number 7, which is the coldest setting. They set it back to number 3. The following day, they got up and again their food was frozen. The setting was back to number 7. That night, the mother decided to keep her eyes and ears open for any strange noises. Sure enough, in the wee hours of the morning, she awoke to footsteps in the trailer. She spoke aloud, "Leave the refrigerator alone." The next morning their food was not frozen and the setting stayed at number 3.

The most active trailer is referred to as Trailer 7, the 1951 Royal Mansion. Numerous guests staying in the Royal Mansion have claimed to hear someone walking through the trailer late at night while they are asleep. A common occurrence is the refrigerator door opening and closing by itself, as well as, the cabinets and cupboards in the kitchen. A little plastic sign, which hangs above the stove, is said to have fallen off on different occasions and remains on the floor until guests in the morning put it back. The Aunt of one of the owners stayed in the Royal Mansion while visiting for Thanksgiving. Sure enough, she awoke one night to the cupboards opening and closing. She was too afraid to get up to see what was going on for fear of actually seeing a ghost.

When the owner comes in to stage the trailer for arriving guests, the chenille blanket on the bed is always messed up, as if someone had recently sat on the bed. When she gave me a tour of the Shady Dell, she told me that when we go into the bedroom the blanket would need to be straightened. Sure enough, there was an imprint on the blanket in the middle of the bed and she had to straighten it out. Guests staying at the Royal Mansion also claim to hear a little boy playing tag in the cemetery behind the trailer.

Even though all the trailers have a rich history, and were enjoyed by many families over the years, we are pretty certain that the hauntings are due to the Evergreen Cemetery located just feet away from all the haunted trailers. It should be noted that only the trailers located against the property border between the Shady Dell and the Evergreen Cemetery are considered haunted.

ELDORADO SUITES
Type of Hauntings: Intelligent

HISTORY

The Eldorado Suites sit high on OK Street in Old Bisbee and overlook the infamous Brewery Gulch. Originally built in 1914 to house miners working in the Copper Queen mine, the building was later transformed into one of the first apartment buildings in Arizona. At the time it was built, it consisted of eighteen one-bedroom units that were shared by the miners. In the 1980s the rooms were converted into twelve two-bedroom suites. Many people throughout Bisbee's history have lived at the Eldorado Suites, though the records of who they were have been lost.

PARANORMAL ACTIVITY

There appears to be only one room which is haunted at the Eldorado Suites, and it is that of Room 4. Little history is known about the room, except that the ghost really likes to taunt one of the owners.

The first incident occurred in the summer of 2008. Fiona was in Room 4 carrying a laundry basket of sheets, getting ready to make the bed for new guests checking in. She entered Room 4 from the back patio as the sun was starting to set. As she made her way through the kitchen to the front bedroom, she felt someone push her from behind. At the time, all the guests in the hotel were out enjoying the lovely summer evening in downtown Bisbee. She looked behind her and saw no one. The push was not very hard and we don't think the ghost intended to hurt her. Nonetheless, the owner quickly put down the laundry basket and ran out of the suite.

A couple of months later, she experienced more paranormal activity while she was in the bedroom of Room 4 vacuuming. She witnessed the door between the kitchen and back bedroom swing closed all by itself. She claimed there was no draft in the room and could not find a logical explanation for the occurrence.

Opposite page:
Room 4 of the Eldorado Suites is the only one known to have paranormal activity. *Photo Courtesy of Author.*

Again while in Room 4, Fiona was straightening up the room for guests checking in. She turned the lights on and gathered up the dirty laundry to take them to the hotel's laundry room. Upon her return, the lights, which she had turned on, were now off, and the fan, which was not running, was on full throttle.

It was not long after the last paranormal incident that the Eldorado Suites received the following email from a gentleman who used to live in the building when it was an apartment building.

> *I used to live in #4, back when it was apartments and I was wondering if the haunting had continued since I moved out?*
>
> *Anyway, back when I lived there, the back door used to open frequently, close, then the closet on the side of the master bedroom would open and then close, followed by the one in the kitchen, and then finally the bathroom door would open and close. It was a random event and happened at least six or seven times in the six months that I lived in the apartment. I was a technical director with one of the contractors at the time; but was offered a job, so I moved back home to Atlanta.*
>
> *Three people who worked for me lived in the building and saw these door events, as well as both my parents who came out for a visit*
>
> *Best of luck to you and to Bisbee!*

The owner states that the activity does not scare her too much, and she has never felt threatened in any way—though one must wonder why the spirit chooses to haunt just Room 4. What attachment did they have to the room? And why does it choose to taunt Fiona? Is it because it is familiar with her, since she is at the hotel all the time?

COPPER QUEEN HOTEL
Type of Hauntings: Residual, Intelligent, Shadow Ghost

HISTORY

Construction on the famous Copper Queen Hotel started in 1898 and was completed in 1902, with funds provided by Phelps Dodge. The mining company built the hotel so that its executives and investors had a place to stay that was luxurious and elegant. During construction, they had to blast away part of the mountainside to make room for the building, as well as pump water up the hill from the Phelps Dodge Mercantile, which is now the Convention Center. It is said that there is a secret passageway underneath the hotel that leads to the Convention Center, though we have never been able to locate it.

The Copper Queen Hotel is the oldest continuously running hotel in Arizona.
Photo Courtesy of Author.

The entrance of the hotel is tiled and just recently the hotel has begun uncovering and restoring this historic floor after previous owners glued carpets on top of it. After you enter the hotel there is a sitting room, known as the Palm Room. The original ceiling of the Palm Room was believed to be made of Tiffany Glass. No one is certain why it was replaced, but now it has a wooden vaulted ceiling.

The Copper Queen is the oldest continuously running hotel in the state of Arizona. The original hotel had 73 rooms with shared baths at the end of each hall. After many modern renovations, the hotel now has 48 rooms, each with its own bathroom. In 1944, the hotel installed an elevator, and added a fifth floor to house the elevator equipment. It is in the Elevator Room where we host our weekly Ghost Hunt of the Copper Queen Hotel. The Ghost Hunt is for hotel guests only, and has proven to be quite the Bisbee attraction.

In the mid 1970s the swimming pool was added to the building. This makes the Copper Queen Hotel the only hotel in Bisbee with an elevator and a pool. Room 211 is the John Wayne room, and he is rumored to have thrown Lee Marvin through the saloon window. Other guests who are believe to have stayed at the Copper Queen include General John Pershing, President Teddy Roosevelt, Charlie Chaplin, Fatty Arbuckle, Harry Houdini, Julia Roberts, Keifer Sutherland, Presidential Hopeful Senator McCain and my personal favorite Johnny Depp. The Copper Queen Saloon was originally extremely small and would seat only a dozen people. In the space that is now the rest of the Saloon, there were offices for Western Union and the Chamber of Commerce. The saloon now is home to many local musicians who can be heard playing nightly, as well as a couple of spirits of years gone by.

PARANORMAL ACTIVITY

The Copper Queen Hotel is haunted by over sixteen spiritual entities. The ghost of an older gentleman has been seen in the Teddy Roosevelt Room. He wears a top hat, cape, and has a beard and long hair. His picture has been taken on the fourth floor before he gets scared of the cameras and walks through walls to hide from them. He is also seen walking out of the bathroom in the Teddy Roosevelt Room, around the desk, through the door and then disappears down the hallway.

There is the ghost of a little girl who is seen on the second floor by the entrance to the pool. At one time, the only person we thought to have seen her was the General Manager of the hotel, Adam. Though, after one of our ghost tours, a lady pulled me aside and asked why I hadn't mentioned the ghost of the little girl. I was shocked because I knew that the General Manager rarely spoke of her to anyone. The woman on my tour told me that her mother was staying in a room on the second floor, and saw the apparition of a little girl that she described as looking like Shirley Temple. A psychic who was visiting the Copper Queen told the General Manager that the little girl ghost is looking for her parent's room and is very lost. She showed herself to the manager because she knows she can trust him.

The Smoking Man is one of the most frequently smelled ghosts in Arizona. He enjoys haunting the Copper Queen Hotel, especially the third and fourth floors. When people see him, The Smoking Man is dressed in a top hat and a cape, and he has gray stringy hair. He is often seen smoking a cigar and usually smells like one, too. Guests will see him and then smell his cigar smoke. They will also smell cigar smoke waft down the hallways of the hotel, or through their rooms. The reason why he favors the third floor is because that is where the smoking balcony used to be. It was the spot where he would hang out with is friends and colleagues, smoke cigars, drink brandy, and discuss politics. His spirit is active on the fourth floor because that is where the upstairs office is located and we believe he was some sort of bookkeeper or accountant at the hotel. Though, he is smelled and seen on all the floors of the building.

The most active ghost in all of Bisbee is Billy. He was a little boy between the ages of five and eight when he died. Billy is thought to have drowned in the San Pedro River. His spirit came back to the hotel because his mother or close family member, at the time of his death, was working there. Billy is the most playful of the Copper Queen's Ghosts. He has been seen jumping on the leather couch in the lobby and people hear him laughing in the hallways. He loves to pick up and examine shinny objects. He never steals them. He places them in different areas than where they were put down originally or he puts them back upside down, or turned around. He also enjoys the candy that guests leave on their nightstands. He has taken the candy of many guests, and leaves only the wrappers as a "thank you."

There is a story of a family eating with their little girl at the Copper Queen's restaurant. The daughter kept looking under the table. When her parents asked her what she was looking at, her response was, "the little boy under the table." When the parents looked to see the little boy, he had disappeared. Another couple that was eating at the Winchester had just finished their meal. The wife put her crumpled napkin on the table. She and her husband, along with the surrounding tables, watched as the napkin smoothed itself and moved to the other side of the table.

Billy's Room, which was named after him to honor the Copper Queen's famous ghost. *Photo Courtesy of Author.*

Once, a family with three children was staying in the hotel. This made Billy happy because he thought he had children to play with; except, the children were preoccupied with watching TV and would rather do that than play with a ghost they didn't know was there. Billy started to play with the volume on their television to get their attention, but to no avail. Billy turned off their TV hoping that would get their attention, but the children just turned it back on again. Ultimately, he unplugged it from the wall, and that finally got the kids attention.

Billy is afraid of water, and some patrons say that they can hear a boy cry when they run their tub water or take a shower.

The most popular Copper Queen ghost is that of Julia Lowell, who was a woman of the evening. One theory is that Julia's father was either the manager of the hotel or owned it at one point. He knew of his daughter's occupation; but would rather she work under his roof than on the streets. Another theory is that Julia lived at the Copper Queen during the Depression. The hotel was said to rent out its rooms, like apartments, to help supplement its income. Either way, we know that Julia lived at the Copper Queen and made her living entertaining men.

The story goes that Julia fell madly in love with one of her customers who was a married man. She confessed her love for him. In response, he spurned her, and told her to leave him alone. He was not going to leave his wife for a mere prostitute. Julia's overreaction to this was that she decided to take her own life. Local folklore states that Julia hung herself in the hotel; many believe she hung herself in the hallway outside of Room 315. Julia has become such a popular ghost at the Copper Queen Hotel that they dedicated Room 315 in her honor. It is now known as the Julia Lowell Room.

Julia loves to taunt men staying at the hotel. She will dance a seductive dance at the foot of their beds, pull blankets off their feet and tickle their toes, and whisper in their ears while they sleep. She has also been seen on the main staircase wearing scant clothing and holding a bottle. She usually smells like old lilac perfume.

Employees of the Copper Queen have seen other ghosts, and have experienced other paranormal activities. One employee, who has worked there for years, said that while she was growing up in Bisbee, the local ghost story of the Copper Queen Hotel involved the ghost of a woman dressed in black Victorian clothes. She would descend the staircase, survey the lobby, and then walk back up the staircase. Other employees have seen her as well, standing on the first set of stairs heading up to the second floor.

There has been seen a shadow walking back and forth by the entrance to the restaurant, after the restaurant is closed down and dark. It looks like a male figure, though no details of his face or body can be seen. In the far left corner of the restaurant, a ghost of what is believed to be a cowboy, has been seen relaxing in a chair and smoking what appears to be a cigar.

Julia Lowell's room. Many believe she killed herself in the hallway outside this room. *Photo Courtesy of Author.*

On the third floor, employees have seen a mist between Rooms 314 and 315, which is the Julia Lowell Room. The mist is described as gray in color and almost takes up the width of the hallway. When one of the employees saw it, it immediately moved and went through the wall. It never appears threatening or scary. It is most likely ectoplasmic mist.

Employees have also seen a woman on the stairs. One employee saw her every other day for a period of about a week. Every time he saw her, she would come further down the staircase. He said that he could only see her from the waist down and that she was wearing a dark beige skirt. Once, he was talking to another employee who was sitting behind the front desk; he was in front of the desk and in the reflection of the mirror that sits on the wall behind the desk, he saw this ghost's reflection. At first, he thought it was the reflection of a co-worker, but when he turned around, no one was there. Other employees have seen the ghost of the lady on the stairs as well. One employee saw her walk down the stairs halfway, then turn around and walk back up. This employee described her as wearing a white high-collar blouse, black skirt with old fashion keys hanging off it and holding a lantern.

While working the night audit in the front office, an employee claimed to hear loud footsteps coming from the second-floor mezzanine. Since it was late at night, he wanted to make sure no one was running around the building causing a ruckus and disturbing the other guests. When he got to the second floor, there was no one there. During its many years of operation, it is believed that the Copper Queen's second floor was used both as an extension of the hospital, which was located across the street during the Indian War, and also used as the telephone operators' quarters when phones were first brought to Bisbee.

This same employee stated that he has heard his name being called while in the downstairs office. One night in 2007, he smelled smoke, and went out from behind the front desk to see if he could tell where the smell was coming from. He heard a low deep growl that didn't sound threatening, but it still caught him off guard. He went back into the office and a short time later heard noises coming from the lobby. He went out to see what it was and heard a male voice say, "Good morning." During one of his nightly walks through the hotel, at 11 p.m. he was on the fourth floor and heard what sounded like a desk bell ring twice outside Room 408. As he descended and entered the third floor, he heard a little boy's voice say, "Hello," from behind him.

Numerous employees who work the front desk have smelled perfume behind the desk, and many believe it to be that of Julia. Many have heard voices as well as seen a shadow walk in the restaurant.

The Saloon has its own set of paranormal activities. One employee was sitting at the table all the way in the back of the saloon, when he felt someone standing next to him on his right side. He could see the person out of his peripheral vision and could tell that he was wearing a white button down shirt and beige pants. He looked over to say hello to whoever it was, and the figure had disappeared. This happened again to the same employee some time later. He was sitting at the same table having a drink with some friends when he saw the same ghost on his right hand side out of his peripheral vision. At the same time he felt the ghost's cold hand press down on his left shoulder, sending goose bumps up and down his body.

Female bartenders have felt the ghost of a man watching them from the liquor cabinet. When one of the bartenders confronted another one and said that every time she walks past the liquor cabinet it feels as though someone is watching her, her co-worker confirmed that many times females in the bar have stated the same thing.

The back of the Copper Queen's bar where many employees have had unexplained phenomena occur. *Photo Courtesy of Author.*

While walking past the cabinet the same female bartender said that she heard a male voice go "ummmm" in a chauvinistic type of way. She has also heard a knocking coming from the cabinet and notes that the mirror that hangs by it is always askew. She will fix it and it will hang crooked again. She has also heard what sounds like a man sitting at the stool by the end of the bar, and when she goes over to help them, the stool will be empty. Lights have gone on and off, and sometimes she hears a female calling her name and no one will be there. Additionally, she has heard tapping on the glass windows of the saloon after she has closed up and is walking down the street heading for home.

GHOST HUNT

Every Thursday night I conduct a Ghost Hunt of the Copper Queen Hotel. Hotel guests are allowed and encouraged to join me. We turn off all the lights on the fourth floor, and open all the unoccupied rooms. I give guests a tour of the haunted fourth floor and explain some of the paranormal activity that has taken place there. I instruct the guests on how to use ghost hunting equipment such as EMF Detectors, K2 Meters, Dowsing Rods, Pendulums, Compasses and the proper way to take photographs during a ghost hunt. Guests are permitted and encouraged to use our equipment while on the hunt. If guests bring their own Digital Voice Recorders, I show them how to catch proper EVPs and instruct them on how to act when someone is recording EVPs. All these are described in the "So You Want to be a Ghost Hunter" chapter of this book.

Every week we have had multiple paranormal experiences. We get readings on our EMF or K2 Meters, the Dowsing Rods cross, photographs are taken, or someone sees or hears something out of the ordinary. Room 401 has proven to be the most active room during our ghost hunts. On multiple occasions we have used the K2 Meter and Dowsing Rods to communicate with the spirits, and more often then not, we get responses. We have also experienced girls getting their hair tugged, vibrations while guests have been sitting on the bed, hands being touched, and knocks on the wall.

On numerous occasions while on the Ghost Hunt at the Copper Queen Hotel I have seen a tall man outside of Room 409. He wears a coat and is so tall that he blocks out the light from the exit sign that is outside of the room. When I have seen him, he is always walking from Room 409, down the hallway towards Billy's room. When he is spotted, we are usually standing either outside of Billy's room or the Teddy Roosevelt room. Once, while standing by Billy's room, two other girls on the Ghost Hunt that evening spotted him at the same time I did. On that occasion, he walked from Room 409, down the hallway towards the Teddy Roosevelt room.

In Billy's Room, Room 412, guests have seen an indentation on the chair as if someone was sitting down on it, and at the same time they could feel a cold spot. In Billy's Room we will usually get high EMF readings that will be there one minute and then disappear the next. After trying to track down the EMFs to an electrical source, and finding none, we have to conclude that it is paranormal. In Room 413, guests have witnessed the fan start spinning very slowly after asking for a sign from the spirits. Others have smelled both Julia's perfume and the Smoking Man's cigars while venturing down the darkened hallway. When children come on the Ghost Hunt we are sure to get lots of activity. Children have been more likely to make contact with the spirits of Billy and the little girl ghost. Numerous photographs have been taken which contain lights, mists, and unexplainable distortions.

SO YOU WANT TO BE A GHOST HUNTER

You have read the stories, you have done the historic research, you have seen the TV shows and now you want to try your hands at ghost hunting.

What is your next step? To go on an actual ghost hunt!!

I will tell you from experience there is nothing more spine tingling then being in a haunted location, with the lights off and not knowing what will happen. Though it is fun, it should be something that you take very seriously. You will be searching for the unknown, unexplainable, and sometimes dangerous. In this chapter I will explain the basic equipment you need to get started, as well as protocols you should follow when going on an investigation. Remember that in the Paranormal Field there are no experts! This is a field we know little about. Therefore, everything in this chapter should be used as guidelines, rather than rules. If you find a method or instrument that works better than those I have listed below, by all means use it! You might find a breakthrough in this field that investigators have been looking for!

Equipment

- Notebook and pencil (mechanical)
- Flashlight
- Compass
- Watch
- Walkie Talkies
- Sketch pad to draw maps and diagrams
- Bait (coins, ball, toys, any thing small and shiny)
- Hair ties (to pull back hair when taking photographs)
- Extra Batteries!!!
- Camera (digital or 35 mm) and extra film/memory cards

- Digital or analog audio recorder with external microphone (try to get one that hooks up to your computer via a USB port)
- Video Camera (digital or video)
- EMF Detector
- K2 Meter
- Tripod for Cameras and Video Cameras
- Thermometer
- Infrared Camera
- Dowsing Rods
- Pendulum
- Baby Powder
- Motion Sensor Lights
- Case to store all your equipment in

Notebook and Mechanical Pencil

It is very important to keep a notebook with you at all times during an investigation. You can use it to write down notes on the weather, temperature, EMF readings, and anything you experience firsthand. Make sure your pencils are mechanical because you do not want to carry around a pencil sharpener on a ghost hunt! If you experience any anomaly, record it in your notebook for future reference.

Flashlight
Always bring a flashlight with you on an investigation. Most of the time ghost hunts take place at night, after it is dark. Using a flashlight will make sure you don't hurt yourself, your partners, or your equipment! Always bring extra batteries for your flashlights, too, as ghosts like to use batteries to help manifest themselves. It is not uncommon for batteries to be drained during an investigation.

Compass
A compass can be used as an inexpensive EMF detector. When there is a high Electro Magnetic Field the compass will keep spinning and be unable to find north. To use it, stand still and allow the compass to find north. If it is unable to, you know you are in an EMF field and should start taking notes and

photographs. A spirit may be close. Make sure your compass has a free spinning needle. Keep the compass as flat and level as possible, though it will bounce around as you walk. If the needle starts to move away from NORTH, take note of it. The needle should always be pointing NORTH. Make sure there is no magnetic interference such as electrical outlets. If you can't find any, continue to take notes on how much the needle points off of NORTH.

Watch

You will want to keep track of the time, and make note of when you have a personal experience.

Walkie Talkies

If you are in a huge building, or have half your crew outside, so as to not have human contamination during your investigation, it is a good idea to carry with you a set of Walkie Talkies. They will keep your team in constant communication with one another. We have also found that spirits like to communicate using them!

Sketch Pad

Use your sketchpad to make diagrams of the location's floor plan. Use this diagram as a reference when taking your base readings.

Bait

Bait can be coins, toys, jewelry, keys, flashlights, or anything else that might attract a spirit, and therefore cause you to collect more evidence. Place the bait in a location where a ghost or spirit is known to haunt. Make sure you announce out loud to the spirit that the object is there for them to play with. See what happens!

Hair Ties

When on an investigation, you will be taking photographs. While taking these photographs, make sure your hair is always pulled back. Otherwise you risk getting hair in front of the lens. What you think might be a ghost in your photo might really be your own hair!

Extra Batteries

One of the theories about ghosts is that when they manifest they try to suck energy from sources around them. Usually this energy can be found in batteries. It is not uncommon while on a ghost hunt to have your batteries drained from your cameras or other equipment that uses them. This is why we strongly recommend bringing extra batteries with you. You will also want to start each investigation with fresh batteries in all your devices.

Camera

When on a ghost hunt some people prefer to use an old school 35mm camera. The benefit to this is that you will have a negative of all the photos you have taken. The advantage of having a negative is if there is something paranormal in the photo, it is easier to prove to a skeptic that the photo has not been manipulated in any way. When using a film camera, I recommend getting a higher speed film if you will be photographing at night.

Ghost hunters and paranormal investigators use digital cameras more than they do film cameras. The digital camera has all the benefits of a film camera; and, in the long run, is less expensive, as there are no development costs and no film costs. When using your digital camera, be sure to set it on the highest quality setting possible. If you catch a ghost in a photo, you will want to be able to zoom in to see what you caught! It might be beneficial to get a digital camera that works with infrared lights (IR). That way if you are using an IR recorder, or IR lights to illuminate a room ,your camera will be able to make use of the IR as well.

Always remember to make sure to pack extra memory cards or extra film!

When taking photographs always, always, always put the strap of the camera around your wrist or around your neck. Two reasons for this; first off you do not want to drop your camera. Second, you do not want the strap to fall in front of your lens. This would result in you taking a photograph of what you think is a ghost, which, in actuality, would just be your camera strap! Also note where your fingers are when taking a photograph. Make sure they are not in front of your lens! Prior to taking photos, let your camera acclimate to the temperature by taking it out of its case and letting it sit for a half hour or so. When in cold weather, hold your breath while taking a photograph. Also, do not smoke while taking a photo or stand around anyone who is smoking. This would result in a ghostly object appearing in your picture which in fact is just smoke.

Prior to your first photograph, clean the lens of your camera with a lens cloth. As you are taking photographs, take notes regarding any weather conditions such as dust, fog, rain, or snow, as well as, any reflective surfaces off which your flash might reflect.

How do you know when to take a photograph on a paranormal investigation? When you are getting high readings off your EMF, K2, when the dowsing rods cross, or when you just get that gut instinct to start shooting!

Remember that when you are inside a dark location the flash from your camera may blind your fellow ghost hunters. This is why we always say, "Flash," before the camera takes the photo. Thus, your friends will know not to look directly at you while you are taking the photograph and therefore won't be blinded.

Digital or Analog Voice Recorder

This is a great tool when doing EVP work. EVP stands for Electronic Voice Phenomenon and is a technique ghost hunters use very often. They will have a recording session during an investigation and try to catch a disembodied voice on the recording. A digital recorder can cost anywhere from $30, all the way up to $200. Those with external microphones work best on ghost hunts. Some models come with a USB port directly on the recorder for easy hookups to a computer.

When you are doing an EVP session, it is crucial to take an audible note of any naturally occurring sounds in the building, such as a water heater, toilet, or refrigerator. Note these sounds in your notebook and make sure to refer back to these notes when you are listening to your recording.

When you get to a haunted location, place your recording device on a flat surface. If you try to walk around with it, you will get too much background noise from your walking, your clothing moving, and air moving past the recorder. If you have an external microphone, place it at least three feet from your recording device. If you are using a recorder that needs a cassette tape, make sure to use a fresh unused tape at the beginning of any session. Never reuse an old tape! Reusing tapes can cause many false positives as the previous data is not completely erased.

Most ghost hunters find that the best way to catch an EVP is to do what is known as a Question Answer Session. Once your recorder is set up properly, start asking questions to the spirits. This will feel really strange at first, but you will soon get used to it. Allow a couple of seconds between asking questions to allow for the spirit to give you an answer.

Here are a few sample questions you can ask.

What is your name?
How old are you?
Why are you here?
Do you like it here?
What year is it?

While doing an EVP session, if you or another investigator makes any sort of noise; a burp, cough, sneeze, stomach growl, or fart, make a verbal note of it so that when you are analyzing your recording, you don't think it is something paranormal. The same goes for any noises such as a car driving by, an alarm going off, thunder or rain. Always make a verbal note of it.

One last word of advice while recording EVPs, never under any circumstances, should you or anyone else with you during the investigation, whisper during a session. Your whisper might be picked up by the recorder and analyzed as a disembodied voice. Again never, ever whisper!

Video Camera

A video camera with IR capability or night vision works best on ghost hunts, presuming you will be in the dark. Make sure to recharge extra batteries and to bring extra tapes. If your group is sophisticated enough, you can hook your digital video cameras into a DVR system. The DVR system will hold your recordings on its memory, as well as file it for your for easy reference. When you are reviewing your video footage, it is very important to do so in real time. Do not fast forward through the tape, hoping that if there was anything paranormal that you would see it, chances are that you wouldn't! Some paranormal activity takes a split second and then it is gone. If you are not watching the video in real time, you could miss what could be potential evidence!

EMF Detector

EMF stands for Electro Magnetic Field or Frequency, and it is a device that will measure the fluctuations in Electro Magnetic Fields. One theory is that when a spirit tries to manifest itself, it will gather energy from around it; therefore, creating its own electro magnetic field. The EMF Detector will pick up the fluctuations. The first thing you want to do is put fresh batteries in your EMF detector. This will guarantee that the device is working properly. When you get a spike on your EMF detector, it is vital that you try to first find a natural occurrence for the EMF. Electro Magnetic Fields are all around us, in wires, TVs, alarm clocks, computers, and even humans have their own EMF field. If you are unable to find a naturally occurring EMF field, it is then safe to presume that your spike might be paranormal. At this point it would be a good idea to start taking photographs or to try an EVP session.

K2 Meter

A K2 Meter is a type of EMF Detector. It is designed with lights that go off when there is a strong Electro Magnetic Field. Paranormal investigators will use the K2 Meter as a communication tool, asking the spirit to walk up to it and light up the lights. They will instruct the ghost on how it works, and then tell it to light up the lights to answer *yes* or *no* to their questions.

Camera Tripod

It is always a good idea to bring a tripod with you on a hunt. You can set the tripod up in a corner of the room and let your video camera record without you having to be in the room. For photography cameras, it is a good idea to use your tripod if you are taking a long exposure shot without a flash. It will prevent you from getting blurs in your photos, as the tripod will hold your camera steadier then you can hold it in your hand.

Thermometer

One theory is that when a ghost tries to manifest itself, it will gather energy from around it, therefore creating either a warm or cold spot. A thermometer is essential for measuring these temperature fluctuations. When you purchase a thermometer try to get one with an ambient air feature as well as an IR feature.

This will allow you to take the temperatures of both the air around the cold/warm spot and surface temperatures of objects around the cold/warm spot.

Infrared Camera

You can obtain an infrared camera from most gadget shops that have a security section. Online stores such as staples.com and target.com have an affordable selection to choose from as well. The video camera uses infrared lights to be able to capture images in total darkness. On ghost hunts this comes in handy because the camera might pick up a ghost that we cannot see due to the dark. Most infrared video cameras can be hooked up to a TV with a VCR, DVR, or even your computer. As with regular video, it is essential that you analyze any and all video recordings in real time.

Dowsing Rods

Dowsing Rods are used mostly to find underground water sources, though they are used to find paranormal activity as well. The rods work as an antenna that picks up vibration frequencies. Metaphysical ghost hunters use dowsing rods more than scientific ghost hunters. Though there is nothing that says they can't be incorporated into the scientific approach of paranormal investigating as well. As you hold the Dowsing Rods, allow them to move freely in your hands. Keep your elbows bent and wrists close to your chest. Angle the rods down just a little, so they are weighted. As you walk, your rods might cross, open, or point in one direction. At this point you might want to start taking photographs or start doing EVP work. You can also ask questions to the spirits and have them answer through the way they cross the rods. For instance, you can ask the spirit to cross the rods for a *yes* answer and to uncross them for a *no* answer. You can also have the spirits point the rods in certain directions to help you locate where they are.

Pendulum

A Pendulum is another metaphysical way to search and communicate with an entity. Usually pendulums are made of crystals that can be dangled from a chain or string, though I have heard of people using their necklaces and key chains as pendulums as well. The pendulum will swing in one direction or the other indicating an answer to a question that has been asked. Make sure when using a pendulum, that it is your own and not someone else's. When you purchase your pendulum allow the pendulum to pick you. You will know when you have found the right one! Also make sure it is cleansed before you use it for the fist time. You can cleanse it by placing the pendulum outside in the sun for an entire day; as the sun sets take it inside. You can also run it under a water faucet or stream as you visualize all the bad negative energy being washed away. After you have cleansed your pendulum, make sure to establish its directional swing. Ask it to show you *yes*, and it will swing in one direction. Ask it then to show you *no*, and it will swing in another direction. Take note of these, for your pendulum is showing you how to communicate with it. At this point, when you feel there is an entity present, you can start asking yes or no questions, and your pendulum will respond.

Baby Powder

Baby powder can be useful to have in your ghost hunting tool kit. Though it can be a bit messy, an investigator can use it to try to find footprints, handprints, or to see if objects have moved. If there is an area where an entity is seen walking through, simply sprinkle some baby powder on the floor (please don't do this on carpet) and leave the vicinity. Make sure other investigators on your team know not to walk in that area. Come back later during the investigation and see if there are any footprints in the powder. If a spirit is known to move objects, use bait and place it on a thin layer of baby powder. If the powder around the objects is disturbed, you might want to investigate further, for the ghost might have moved the objects and therefore disrupted the baby powder. Just make sure to clean up the baby powder after the investigation is over!

Motion Sensor Lights

Motion Sensor Lights are good to use if you will be in the room or area where the activity is expected. Simply set up any sort of motion sensor light, which you can usually purchase at any home goods store for a reasonable price, and wait. When the light goes on, and you cannot visibly see anything that would make it go off, start to take photographs and do EVP work. An unseen presence may be with you!

Case To Store Your Equipment In

Use a case which is sturdy and strong and that can fit most of your equipment comfortably. You can use anything from an old briefcase, to a custom-made storage case. Just know that you will be spending lots of money on your ghost hunting equipment and you want it to stay safe. Therefore, don't hesitate to spend a few extra dollars on a storage case that will keep your equipment safe, clean, and dry!

Ghost Hunting Protocols

There are many guidelines we follow as Ghost Hunters and Paranormal Investigators. These will keep you and your team out of trouble and out of harms way. It will also give your team a sense of professionalism when dealing with a client.

- Never, under any circumstances are you to trespass on property you are not allowed to go onto. Always get permission to do an investigation on property that is not your own. This is true even if you are staying in a haunted hotel. Make sure the hotel is aware that you will be up at night, walking the hallways, with your equipment. Most of the time haunted hotels will encourage you to investigate their most haunted spots and share with you some of their personal stories.

- As soon as you get to a new location to investigate, make sure you map it out on your graph paper. This is a good time to take a base reading of the property with your EMF meter and thermometers. Always do this in the daylight, so you get a feel for the property before you turn off the lights. Some call this the Preliminary Investigation.

- Interview anyone who has experienced the paranormal activity to get their stories and to find out where the most active parts of the building are located.

- Make sure that no one in your group is wearing cologne, perfume, or fragrant deodorant. Some ghosts have scents that you can actually smell. If a group member is wearing any scents themselves, it might be mistaken for the spirit.

- When doing your Preliminary Investigation make sure to take note of any surfaces in the building that might be reflective. Camera flashes will reflect off such surfaces and what you might think is an anomaly, might really be your camera flash reflecting off a shiny surface.

- Make sure that any photos taken or any EVPs recorded are not altered or enhanced in any way during your analysis.

- It is very important not to disclose any evidence you think you might have caught with the property owners until it has been fully analyzed!

- Never, under any circumstances, should investigators or ghost hunters be under the influence of drugs or alcohol.

- Nothing should be taken off the premises as souvenirs.

- All members must be in groups of two or more while on an investigation. Two reasons for this. One is safety. The other is, if you witness something, there are two of you to back up your story.

- Keep the property owner away from the investigation. You don't want them to get in the way, or to tamper with evidence.

- Always try to find a natural occurrence for noises or high EMF readings before classifying it as paranormal.

- Always, under all circumstances, be professional and well behaved. If you see a ghost or spirit, do not go screaming out of the building. Stay put and try to capture evidence.

Question Log to Ask Property Owners

Here are some questions you might want to ask the property owners. This should be done during the Preliminary Investigation. One member of your group can be asking these questions while others are setting up equipment. Always remember to act professional when asking the questions and do not react in a negative way to any of the answers. Simply write them down in your notebook.

- Address of property?
- Year it was built?
- History of site?
- Any recent remodeling?
- Any occupants drinking alcohol or doing mind altering drugs?
- Any occupants involved in the occult?
- What paranormal occurrences are happening?
- Who has witnessed these occurrences?
- Any strange odors in the property?
- Any strange odors associated with the occurrences?
- Have any voices been heard?
- Have any objects been moved?
- Have there been any warm or cold spots in the property?
- Have there been any electrical appliances that are not working property?
- Have there been any plumbing issues?
- Is anyone associated with the property having nightmares or trouble sleeping?
- Are pets or animals acting strangely?
- When was the first paranormal occurrence, what happened, who was involved?
- Have there been other witnesses to the occurrences?
- How often does an occurrence happen?
- Is it threatening?
- What do the property owners suspect is the culprit to the occurrences?

After the interview, it is sometimes helpful for the property owners to lead you through the property pointing out all the paranormal hot spots. Make sure to make notes regarding everything they say happens in each location. These notes will be helpful to you when you go back to set up your equipment, and while you are analyzing it.

After the Preliminary Investigation and after the equipment has been set up, you can turn off the lights and start the Secondary Investigation. This is the fun part, where you get to walk around trying to collect evidence.

When you get high readings on your EMF equipment, or dowsing rods, or pendulum, it is time to try to find a natural source. If there is none, then it is time to take photographs and to do an EVP session. Remember to talk slowly and to allow time between questions for the spirit to answer. Remember to always stay with another investigator and to never wander alone. After you have collected your evidence, call it a night.

I always make it a rule to thank the spirits and ghosts after an investigation and to tell them that they must stay where they are and to not follow me home. Believe it or not, spirits can attach themselves to human beings and travel with them.

Make sure you are refreshed and ready to review your photos, video footage, and EVP recordings. It is necessary to watch video and listen to audio recordings in real time, so that you don't accidentally skip over what could be potential paranormal evidence.

After you have collected your evidence, you can go to the property owner and disclose what you have found. Sometimes they will react to their location being haunted in a positive way, sometimes in a negative way. If they do not want the unwelcome spirit in their home or establishment, you can cleanse the place by using sage (see section following), or you can get a clergyman to bless the building. Usually, if the property owner simply says out loud that the spirit is not welcomed there and to move on, they will find that the spirit will listen and the paranormal activity will stop. If they don't mind the ghosts and just wanted more information about them, then you have done your job.

How to Sage A Building.

Donna Amalong, who was raised by her great aunt who was half Cherokee Indian, states that saging is a good way to get ride of any negative energy as well as ghosts or spirits. She says to get a bundle of sage and light it, direct the sage smoke with either your hand or a feather into all the nooks and crannies of the building or room. She states that to it is very important to sage in the closets, attic, storage areas, basement and behind appliances and furniture.

BIBLIOGRAPHY

2000-2007
<http://www.manninghouse.com/about_us.htm>

2002
<http://www.ghost-trackers.org/bufordhouse.htm>

2007
<http://www.arizonaghosttowntrails.com/brunckowscabin.html>
<http://www.foxtucsontheatre.org/history/>

2008
<http://www.bisbeeinn.com/pages/history.htm>
<http://www.hotelcongress.com/hotel-congress/hotel-history/>

2009
<http://hauntsofamerica.blogspot.com/2007/08/haunting-of-tombstone-arizona-part-one.html>
<http://jamesmorrisstudio.com/miltonhouse.html>
<http://thetombstonemuseum.com/history.htm>
<http://www.royalelizabeth.com/landmark//
<http://www.azparks.gov/Parks/TOCO/index.html>

"Charles Rivers Drake, A Glimpse of a Renaissance Man." *Downtown Tucsonan*. Feb. 2008: 27.
Goodwyn, Melba. *Ghost Worlds*, Woodbury, MN: Llewellyn Publications, 2007.
Price, Ethel Jackson. *Images of America BISBEE*. Chicago, IL: Arcadia Publishing, 2004.
Warren, Joshua. *How To Hunt Ghosts*. New York, NY: Fireside, 2003.
Weiser, Kathy. (2007) "John Heath and the Bisbee Massacre." <http://www.legendsofamerica.com/we-johnheath.html>

Useful Websites

www.ArizonaGhostTours.net
www.OldBisbeeGhostTour.com
www.TucsonGhostTour.com
www.TombstoneGhostTour.com
www.HearseTour.com
www.ICPIR.org

Become a fan of ours on Facebook. Look for Arizona Ghost Tours for the latest on our Ghost Tours, Hearse Tours, Paranormal Weekends, and Copper Queen Ghost Hunts!

MORE SCHIFFER TITLES

www.schifferbooks.com

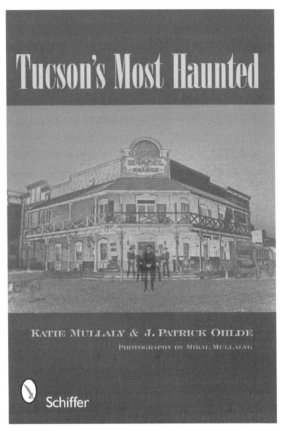

Tucson's Most Haunted. Katie Mullaly and J. Patrick Ohlde. Tucson is one haunted town. From furniture stores and ice cream shops, to an entire community buried beneath a downtown neighborhood, ghosts are everywhere. Who is the ghostly Victorian Lady that glides down the staircase at Z Mansion in historic downtown Tucson? What happened when a rock-throwing ghost suddenly appeared at Fort Lowell over 100 years ago? What became of all the bodies buried in the Court Street Cemetery? Who is responsible for the phantom voices at Old Tucson? Find out, as Tucson's top paranormal investigators give you a peek into the lives of the ghosts who exist alongside Tucsonans, right here in the Old Pueblo!
Size: 6" x 9" • 27 b/w photos • 160 pp.
ISBN: 978-0-7643-3153-4 • soft cover • $14.99

OTHER SCHIFFER TITLES
www.schifferbooks.com

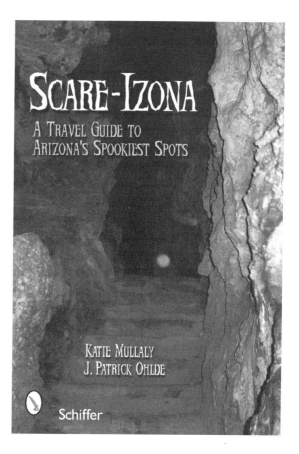

Scare-izona: A Guide to Arizona's Legendary Haunts. Katie Mullaly & J. Patrick Ohlde. Tour 16 of the most haunted locations Arizona has to offer. Make friends with the ghost girl who watches over visitors at the Bisbee Inn. Meet average people who stay at the Oliver House, but then astral project along the quiet-night streets. Hear voices and footsteps of ghosts who prowl the Noftsger Hill Inn. The destinations in this book have impressive paranormal activity that are likely to give you your own spooky stories to tell, if not scare the pants off you!
Size: 6" x 9" • 33 b/w photos • 224 pp.
ISBN: 978-0-7643-2844-2 • soft cover • $14.95

Ghosts in the Cemetery: A Pictorial Study. Stuart L. Schneider; Photography by Rebecca Benjamin. A book unlike any other ghost book -- These are not the typical orb or streak-type ghosts that ghost hunters often get, but full formed, vaporous apparitions. The large color photos are evocative and draw you in as if you are actually standing there and seeing what the photographer saw and felt. The question asked of photographer Rebecca Benjamin is: Are the photographs real? The answer? Yes! In many cultures, spirits of the dead return to visit. They return when the "veil," or separation between life and death and past and present, is at its thinnest. This is the time that Rebecca has taken most of her photographs over the past fifteen years. Ghost stories accompany each cemetery visited. A personal travel guide and pictorial review of haunted cemeteries, including those in New York, New Jersey, Pennsylvania, Massachusetts, Connecticut, New Hampshire, Maine, and Canada.
Size: 11" x 8 1/2" • 70 color photos • 136 pp.
ISBN: 978-0-7643-2988-3
• soft cover • $19.99

Ghosts of Central Arizona. Heather Woodward. Foreword by Mark Boccuzzi; Stacy Fortson, photographer
. From bootleggers and supernatural deaths to ghoulish legends and magical vortexes, this ghostly tour of Central Arizona is an entertaining — and scary — trip. Visit the Jerome Grand Hotel, and stay in one of their "Death Rooms." Travel through vortexes at Bell Rock and Boynton Canyon. Learn about ghost sightings at the Chapel of the Holy Cross and, if you get hungry, the Haunted Hamburger serves up a good ghost tale. Visit Superstition Mountain to Flagstaff, with just a touch of a "Hollywood in Arizona" legend thrown in for good measure. Come along for the ride...if you dare.
Size: 6" x 9" • 30 b/w photos • Index • 192 pp.
ISBN: 978-0-7643-3387-3 • soft cover • $14.99

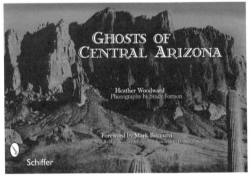